MYSTICISM AND MAGIC IN TURKEY; AN ACCOUNT OF THE RELIGIOUS DOCTRINES, MONASTIC ORGANISATION, AND ECSTATIC POWERS OF THE DERVISH ORDERS

Lucy Mary Jane Garnett

www.GeneralBooksClub.com

Publication Data:

Title: Mysticism and Magic in Turkey; an Account of the Religious Doctrines, Monastic Organisation, and Ecstatic Powers of the Dervish Orders;
Author: Garnett, Lucy Mary Jane, D. 1934
Reprinted: 2010, General Books, Memphis, Tennessee, USA
Original Publisher: New York, C. Scribner's Sons;
Publication date: 1912;
Subjects: Dervishes; Sufism; Religion / Islam / General; Religion / Islam / Sufi; Social Science / Islamic Studies;
BISAC subject codes: REL037000, REL090000, SOC048000,

How We Made This Book for You

We made this book exclusively for you using patented Print on Demand technology.

First we scanned the original rare book using a robot which automatically flipped and photographed each page.

We automated the typing, proof reading and design of this book using Optical Character Recognition (OCR) software on the scanned copy. That let us keep your cost as low as possible.

If a book is very old, worn and the type is faded, this can result in numerous typos or missing text. This is also why our books don't have illustrations; the OCR software can't distinguish between an illustration and a smudge.

We understand how annoying typos, missing text or illustrations, foot notes in the text or an index that doesn't work, can be. That's why we provide a free digital copy of most books exactly as they were originally published. You can also use this PDF edition to read the book on the go. Simply go to our website (www.GeneralBooksClub.com) to check availability. And we provide a free trial membership in our book club so you can get free copies of other editions or related books.

OCR is not a perfect solution but we feel it's more important to make books available for a low price than not at all. So we warn readers on our website and in the descriptions we provide to book sellers that our books don't have illustrations and may have numerous typos or missing text. We also provide excerpts from books to book sellers and on our website so you can preview the quality of the book before buying it.

If you would prefer that we manually type, proof read and design your book so that it's perfect, simply contact us for the cost. Since many of our books only sell one or two copies, we have to split the production costs between those one or two buyers.

Frequently Asked Questions

Why are there so many typos in my paperback?

We created your book using OCR software that includes an automated spell check. Our OCR software is 99 percent accurate if the book is in good condition. Therefore, we try to get several copies of a book to get the best possible accuracy (which is very difficult for rare books more than a hundred years old). However, with up to 3,500 characters per page, even one percent is an annoying number of typos. We would really like to manually proof read and correct the typos. But since many of our books only sell a couple of copies that could add hundreds of dollars to the cover price. And nobody wants to pay that. If you need to see the original text, please check our website for a downloadable copy.

Why is the index and table of contents missing (or not working) from my paperback?

After we re-typeset and designed your book, the page numbers change so the old index and table of contents no longer work. Therefore, we usually remove them. We dislike publishing books without indexes and contents as much as you dislike buying them. But many of our books only sell a couple of copies. So manually creating a new index and table of contents could add more than a hundred dollars to the cover price. And nobody wants to pay that. If you need to see the original index, please check our website for a downloadable copy.

Why are illustrations missing from my paperback?

We created your book using OCR software. Our OCR software can't distinguish between an illustration and a smudge or library stamp so it ignores everything except type. We would really like to manually scan and add the illustrations. But many of our books only sell a couple of copies so that could add more than a hundred dollars to the cover price. And nobody wants to pay that. If you need to see the original illustrations, please check our website for a downloadable copy.

Why is text missing from my paperback?

We created your book using a robot who turned and photographed each page. Our robot is 99 percent accurate. But sometimes two pages stick together. And sometimes a page may even be missing from our copy of the book. We would really like to manually scan each page. But many of our books only sell a couple of copies so that could add more than a hundred dollars to the cover price. And nobody wants to pay that. If you would like to check the original book for the missing text, please check our website for a downloadable copy.

MYSTICISM AND MAGIC IN TURKEY; AN ACCOUNT OF THE RELIGIOUS DOCTRINES,...

PREFACE

My aim in this volume has been to give a thoroughly-impartial account of the Dervishes of Turkey, so far as my knowledge of their principles and practices will allow, neither unduly concealing their lower, nor unduly exalting their higher aspects. And I would fain hope that this brief study of the Mystics of Islam may be found to have not only a speculative and religious, but also a practical and political interest. In controversies with respect to Islam and Civilisation, no account is usually taken of the Mystical side of this Creed as a native element of antagonism to the most essential doctrines of Islam. Widespread as is this unorthodox mysticism, it has been, and still is compelled to keep itself to a certain extent hidden. Events may, however, possibly, sooner or later, bring it to the surface, and endow it with practical significance. For as in the Christian West there has ever been a continuous protest both on the intellectual side by philosophers, and on the rehgious side by mystics, against the more distinctively Semitic doctrines of Christianity, so it has also been in the Moslem East in the Schools of the Dervishes, both among the Persians and the Ottomans. And as this speculative protest by the Monks of Islam has not been without practical results in Persia, so may it likewise be expected to have corresponding results in Turkey. From the Siifism of the Dervish Orders sprang the movement of Babism, the initiation of which was contemporary with the European revolutionary uprising of 48. This movement, which was suppressed with the most barbarous atrocities, gave greater promise than any other event connected with the East of that only possible kind of regeneration–regeneration from within. And should a movement similar to that of Babism, and, like it, derived from the Sufism of the Dervishes, break out in Turkey, its importance will, it is to be hoped, be better understood in Europe than was that of Persian Babism.

L. M. J. G.

A MEVLEVI TEKKEH, SALONICA

A RUFAI, OR " HOWLING " DERVISH

A WANDERING DERVISH

THE ADRIANOPLE GATE, STAMBOUL

BEGGING DERVISH AND NIGHT-WATCHMAN

AN ELDER OF THE MEVLEVI ORDER

MEVLEVI NEOPHYTE LEARNING THE DEVR

A MEVLEVI PLAYER ON THE NEY, OR REED-FLUTE

THE DEVR OF THE MEVLEVI ORDER

A WANDERING DERVISH.

CITY GATE CALLED THE MSVLEVI-HANE STAMBOUL

DERVISH WITH LEANING CRUTCH.

Frontispiece facing page

MYSTICISM AND MAGIC IN TURKEY

CHAPTER I

THE DERVISH ORDERS AND THEIR TENETS

" Under an alien name I shadow One upon whose Head the crown Was, and yet Is, and Shall be; whose Decree The Kingdoms Seven of this world, and the Seas, And the Seven Heavens alike are subject to. All joy to him who, under other name, Instructed us that Glory to disguise To which the initiate scarce dare lift his eyes!"

J AM I, Salaman and Ahsal.

Although the second century of the Mohammedan era has been assigned by various students of the Siifi Philosophy as the date of its origin, societies of mystics would appear to have existed in Islam from its very foundation. For it is recorded that, in the first year of that era, a number of the followers of the Prophet formed themselves into a Brotherhood for the ostensible practice of certain religious exercises of penitence and physical mortification. The word " Dervish " is, in Persian, synonymous with " beggar," and denotes also a person who voluntarily impoverishes himself for the benefit of others. The Khahfs Ali and Abu Bekr, actuated by the desire to fulfil literally that precept of the Koran which says that " He is the best of men who is most useful to his fellow-men," gave up their worldly goods to the common use, and entered upon a career of service to others, calling themselves Safa bashis' to indicate the purity of their lives. The members of these Fraternities took, however, a vow of fidelity to the Prophet and his doctrines, and continued to perform their duties as citizens, meeting occasionally for the performance of the religious exercises peculiar to each congregation. The leaders appointed their successors in office under the title of Khalifeh; and these in their turn transmitted the rule of the Fraternity to the most venerable, or the most spiritually gifted, among its members.

Apart from the attraction of the Siifi doctrines, a life passed in retirement from the world for the purpose of contemplation and devotion appears to have always been congenial to the Oriental mind; and this natural tendency proved stronger than the injunction of the Prophet prohibiting monasticism among his followers. For, even during Mohammed's lifetime, many of the followers of Abu Bekr and All abandoned the rules of the primitive fraternities and formed monastic societies, the first Order of Austere Anchorites being founded in the thirty-seventh year of the Hegira (a. d. 659) by Sheikh Uwais of Yemen, who gave out that the Angel 1 Silvestre de Sacy, Journal des Savants, 1821, p. 724, and DOhsson, Tableau General de la Turquie.

Gabriel had commanded him, in a vision, to withdraw from the world and consecrate himself to a hfe of seclusion and penitence. The celestial visitant at the same time communicated to this ascetic the rules of the Order he was to found, which included abstinence from food, and even the most innocent pleasures, seclusion, and the recital of a great number of prayers by day and night. To these mortifications he voluntarily added the loss of his teeth, requiring the same sacrifice from his disciples, an ordeal which naturally prevented his making proselytes of any but the most fanatical, notwithstanding the Sheikh's high reputation for learning and piety; and the sect never spread beyond Yemen, where it originated. It, however, greatly contributed to the institution of other monastic orders by the more earnestly minded of the followers of Abu Bekr and Ali.

The second century of the Hegira was the era of a great religious movement. On one side was developed a scepticism and unbehef that shook Islam to its foundations, while, on the other hand, mysticism acquired increasing power. This century gave birth to a multitude of sects, and has accordingly been fixed upon, as before mentioned, as the commencement of the system of religion and philosophy professed by the Siifis. Their recognised founder was Abu Said Abulkhair, who hved at the end of that and the beginning of the next century, and founded a monastic institution into which he gathered those whose mode of thinking resembled his own, and laid down rules for their guidance. There is, however, much disparity of opinion as to whether Sufism, as it now exists, was, as asserted by the Sufis themselves, instituted by him. In any case it is probable that the sect did not long remain within the limits of orthodox piety. This was, indeed, impossible. For the Sufi philosophy, as must be admitted, was entirely out of keeping with the creed of Mohammed. And the mysticism of the early Moslems, so tender and full of sentiment, became gradually transformed into Pantheism, an equally natural consequence of its inherent tendencies and of the action upon Islam of older rehgious systems.

In the ninth century of our era, the partisans of this doctrine were divided into two branches, the chief of the one being Abu Yezid, or Bayazid Bestemi, who is revered as the Pir, or founder of the Bestemi Order, and of the other, Djouneid. Bayazid Bestemi openly preached a Pantheism irreconcilable with revealed rehgion, and proclaimed more explicitly than any other Siifi teacher had done the divine nature of man. Among the expressions he made use of are the following:–

"I am an ocean without bottom and without shore, without beginning and without end."

" When men imagine that they are adoring Allah, it is Allah who adores Himself."

" The seed of Siifism was sown in the days of Adam; it sprang up in those of Noah; blossomed under Abraham; and, at the time of Moses the grapes began to be formed. They came to maturity in the days of Jesus, and in those of Mohammed was the wine pressed from them. Those of the Siifis who have loved this Wine have drunk of it until self-consciousness was drowned; and they have then cried, Glory to me! Is there anything greater than I? or I am the truth, there is no God beside me!"i

Djouneid and his followers, on the other hand, while holding practically identical opinions, expressed themselves more prudently, and succeeded in uniting in an extraordinary manner the dogmas of the Koran v dth a system of philosophy which tended to destroy all rehgious practices, and reduce to nothing the merits of faith and works. To arrive at this result they had recourse to an expedient known as the Ketmafiy which has indeed rendered eminent service in all times and in all rehgions, but has been practised with greater success by the Sufis than by any other sect. The terms of the dogmas of Islam were retained, but a totally different signification was given to them by the Sufi teachers. Irreproachable Moslems in outward appearance, these mystics have ever excelled in the art of evading dangerous investigations, and, as M. Dozy remarks, it is rare that an adept, even when in 1 Garcin de Tassy, Mantic Uttair, 4th ed., p. 5; and Sprenger, Journal of the Asiatic Society of Bengal, Vol. Ill, p. 134. Compare also the expressions of St. Augustine, of Duns Scotus Erigena, and of Eckhart, the Christian Mystic (1268-1327). See Vaughan, Hours with the Mystics.

2 Essai Sur IHistoire de IIslamisme, p. 323.

2–(2II9) an ecstatic state, compromises himself by proclaiming in public what is every SM's private behef– am God. " By means of the Ketman and auied methods of propaganda, SMsm has succeeded in permeating every class of Moslem society, has had for centuries past its Chiefs, its Councils, its Monks and its Missionaries, and presents phases varied enough to suit every class of thought. Hosain Ibn Mansur, also called Mansur Halladj, who suffered martyrdom in 922, is revered by the Siifis as one of their greatest saints. He was a disciple of Djouneid, a Persian by birth, and grandson of a Zoroastrian or Magian. According to the moderate Shias, his doctrine was that by practising abstinence, avoiding all worldly pursuits and pleasures, and mortifying the flesh, it is possible for man to elevate himself through successive stages until he becomes the equal of the Elect, and even of the Angels. If he perseveres in this path until nothing remains of his earthly nature, he receives " the Spirit of God " as Jesus is held by Moslems to have received it, and everything that he subsequently does is a divine action. The Shias also maintain that he was put to death on account of the extraordinary influence he exercised among the upper classes, the Princes and their surroundings, which aroused the jealous hostihty of the orthodox clergy. Halladj has not, indeed, been unfavourably judged by the more liberal-minded among orthodox vriters. Gazzah, for instance, who, while he professedly regarded the Sufi philosophy with aversion, expressed his preference for a religion which had its seat in the heart as compared with the dry-orthodoxy expounded by the majority of the Ulema; and he attributed even such assertions of Halladj as I am the Truth, there is nothing in

Paradise save Allah," etc., to his excessive adoration of the Deity. For the majority of orthodox writers of the period, however, this mystic was a blaspheming infidel and sorcerer. On his return to Bagdad after performing the customary pilgrimage to Mekka, strange stories of his miraculous powers were circulated in the city. He was credited with having raised the dead to life; the Djins, it was said, were subject to him, and fulfilled his every command. Fearing his influence with the populace, and incited also, no doubt, by the legists, the Vizier Hamid induced the Khalif Moktadir to place Halladj and his followers at his disposal; and notwithstanding the protection of the Lord Chamberlain, the mystic and his disciples were arrested.

When questioned, the disciples admitted that they looked upon their master as divine, seeing that he had raised the dead to life. But when Halladj himself was interrogated his reply was, "God forbid that I should lay claim to divinity or even to the dignity of Prophet. I am a man who adores the most high God."

The Vizier then summoned the Kadis and principal theologians, and demanded of them a sentence against Halladj. They replied that it was illegal to condemn the accused man without proofs of his alleged crime, as he had not confessed.

Foiled in his design, the Vizier had the mystic brought before him from time to time, and attempted in vain to draw from him some heretical admission. He found at length in his writings a statement to the effect that if a Moslem were prevented making the prescribed pilgrimage to Mekka, he might dispense with it by preparing a chamber in his own house in which to perform the rites connected with that duty; these rites accomplished, he must further take to him thirty orphans, feed them on choice food, clothe them and bestow upon each one seven drachmas; and the fulfilment of these duties would gain for him the merit of having performed the pilgrimage. On this being shown by the Vizier to the Kadi Abou Amr, he was scandalised, and asked, "Where hast thou found such an idea? " Halladj mentioned a work by Hassan of Bassora. "It is a lie! O infidel, whose blood it is lawful to spill," cried the Kadi. The book thou namest was explained to us at Mekka by one of the Doctors; but what thou hast written was not contained in it!"

The Vizier seized eagerly upon the epithet " Infidel," used by the Kadi, and demanded a sentence of death from him. The Kadi at first demurred, saying that such was not his meaning; but the Vizier insisted, and finally obtained a warrant for the execution of Halladj, signed by the Kadi and the other legists. In vain Halladj sought to prove his condemnation unjust. " You have not the right," he exclaimed, " to shed my blood. My faith is that of Islam; I believe in the Hadis (traditions) on which I have written works that may be found at all the booksellers. I have always acknowledged the Four Imams, and the Four Khalifs. I call God to my aid, that my life may be spared!" His protests were unavaiung. The Vizier hastened to bring the fetvas of the legists before the Khauf, who ordered that Halladj should die by scourging. He received a thousand strokes, after which his hands and feet were cut off, and subsequently his head, and his body committed to the flames. The disciples of Halladj, however, refused to believe that their revered master was dead. They maintained that a person resembling him had suffered in his place, and that he would show himself again after forty days. Some declared that they had seen him on the road to Nahrawan, mounted on an ass, and that he had said to them, "Be not hke those foohsh men who believe that I have been scourged and put to death.

Let us now turn to the Sufi version of the story:– " The name of Halladj was in everyone's mouth; they saw the miracles that he did, and an immense multitude followed him. And how should it have been otherwise? Returning from a pilgrimage, he happened to be crossing the desert with four hundred Siifis. His companions said to him one day, We have nothing to eat, and we are hungry; we would like a roast lamb.

(((

Sit down, said the Saint.

" When they were seated, he placed his hand behind his back and gave to each one a roast lamb and two small hot loaves. They ate, and then asked for dates.

Shake me, said the Saint.

" They did so, and there fell from him fresh dates in such quantities that they sufficed for all the company.

" But there were those who were envious of the wonderful gifts of Halladj. These slandered him before the Khahf, and the Doctors of Bagdad condemned him to death because he had said I am the Truth. They desired him to say It is He who is God, and he rephed, Yea, He is all things.

"He was cast into prison. A multitude of people flocked to him for instruction, until, after the lapse of a year, it was forbidden to visit him. The first night of his imprisonment, he was not to be seen in his cell; on the second, neither prisoner nor cell were to be seen. Where hast thou been? demanded the jailer of him. The first night, he rephed, I was with the Glorious Being, for that reason thou sawest me not; on the second, the Glorious Being was with me, so thou sawest neither me nor the cell. To-day I am sent here to satisfy the law; come and do to me what thou art commanded."

It is also related that when he arrived at the prison six hundred persons were confined there. " I will

A RUFAI, OR HOWLING DERVISH deliver you," he said. "Why dehverest thou not thyself? " they asked. " I am in the chains of God, and I have a companion, a faithful guardian. I have only to desire it, and at a sign my fetters will fall from me." He made a sign and the fetters of all the prisoners fell. " But the door is closed," they said. " How shall we depart? " Halladj having made another signal, the doors opened, everyone went out, and he was left alone. " Why departest thou not also? " he was asked. " I have a secret," he replied, " which I must impart only to him who is able to guard a secret."

On the following day the Khahf, learning what had happened, exclaimed, "He will do mischief; let him be hanged!"

They asked Halladj " Where are the prisoners?"

" I have set them free."

" Why hast thou too not departed?"

" Because Allah is offended with me."

The Khahf then gave the order to scourge him. He received six hundred strokes, and at each stroke a voice was heard crying, "Fear nothing, Halladj! " A hundred thousand persons had assembled on the road by which he was to pass to the scaffold. His eyes wandered over them, and he cried, "God I God! God! I am God I"

" What is true love? " a Dervish asked of him.

" That shalt thou learn to-day, to-morrow, and the day after," was the reply.

Give me a remembrance of thee," begged a youth.

The men of this world," replied the martyr, aspire after good works. Do thou aspire after a thing of which an indivisible atom is worth more than the collective good works of angels and men– the knowledge of true science.

While speaking, Halladj danced and waved his hands. What manner of walking is this? he was asked. " Am I not going to the place of my sacrifice? was his reply, and he broke out into the following mystical song:–

Say not, my Friend is heedless of my pain;
The Cup He gives to me He too doth taste.
Like host that with his guest the wine doth drain.
Yet, while the Cup goes round, the block and sword appear.
Such fate is his who with the Dragon drinks.
While ardent shines the summer sun above the plain.

When he placed his foot upon the first step of the scaffold, Halladj exclaimed, "Behold man's ladder to Heaven I" He adjusted his girdle, removed his taiksan–the drapery covering his head and shoulders– turned his face towards Mekka, and with uplifted hands uttered an inaudible prayer. He then mounted the ladder. The people threw stones at him, but he uttered no word of complaint or reproach. When, however, the Siifi Chibli, also a disciple of Djouneid, threw mud at him, he heaved a sigh. " Thou dost not sigh when thou art struck with stones, why sighest thou when they throw but

Evidently signifying that God, being present in the individual, sacrifices Himself.
The Dragon, a sign of the Zodaic, here represents the Deity.

mud at thee? " he was asked. " They who take up stones," repued the martyr, " know not what they do, so that does not afflict me; but Chibu knows that he sins, when he throws but mud." When his hand was cut off, he smiled and said, "It is not difficult to cut off the hand of him who is in chains; it would require greater dexterity to deprive him of the quahties which raise him to the highest heaven." His feet were cut off. He still smiled, saying, "I have still two other feet to carry me to the Two Worlds, cut them off if you can!" When deprived of his hands, he rubbed his cheeks and arms with his bloody wrists; and when questioned as to the meaning of this action, he rephed, "I have already lost much blood, and my cheeks will soon become pale. I am unwilhng you should imagine that they are blanched by terror, and I wish to leave you with rosy cheeks. Dark red is the colour of men." " But why," they persisted, " dost thou besmear thy arms with thy blood? " "I do but perform the ablest i–the ablutions of love should be made with blood."

When he had been deprived of his eyes, and his executioners were preparing to cut out his tongue, he desired to speak once more; and while the mob continued to assail him with stones, he cried, "Great God I Reject them not because they afflict me thus. Praise to Thee, because, for my love of Thee, they have cut off my hands and my feet.

1 The Moslem ablution which precedes the prayers repeated five times daily by all good Moslems.

When my head is severed from my body, grant that I may see Thy face." His last words were, "The only thing required by the Only One, is, that men declare Him to be the Only One."

Such is the version given by the Sufis of the martyrdom of Halladj. They look upon him as one of the most eminent representatives of their doctrines, having shown that death, and above all, the most cruel death, is the happiest thing that can befall a Sufi; for by it his soul is delivered from its prison, the body, and the Lover " attains that " eternal union " with the " Beloved " which he has so long and so ardently desired.

Another legend says that an inspired Siifi asked the Almighty why He permitted Mansiir Halladj to suffer. The reply was, "It is the punishment for the revealer of secrets." It is also related that when the Saint was about to be impaled in addition to his other tortures, the executioners could not perform their duty. In vain they endeavoured to seize him; his body always eluded their grasp, and appeared seated in a composed posture in the air at some distance from the stake. While this was occurring on earth, his soul sought the regions of Paradise. He was accosted by the Prophet, who admitted that he had arrived at the highest stage, that of Wisdl, or " Union," and that his declaration that he was God was true. Mohammed, however, entreated him, for the sake of practical religion, which was necessary for unenlightened mortals, to 1 Dozy, Essai sur IHistoire de VIslamisme, p. 234 et seq.

allow himself to be impaled. The soul of the holy man accordingly, convinced by the words of the Prophet, returned to earth to reanimate his body, and suffer the death to which he had been sentenced by his earthly judges.

Similar conceptions of Oneness with the Deity are expressed in a modern work by a Turkish mystic, of which the following paragraph may serve as an example:–

" And he Jewad laid his head on the pillow of the quest of inspiration. Straightway he opened his eyes, and found himself lying on a shore near a vast city. He rose, and wondering, said to himself, My life! Surely I was in my room. and this city that is before me resembles not ours. There is no strength nor power save in Allah," Am I in a vision? In a single moment poor Jewad forgot all that he had known–those spiritual sciences and strange arts that he had learned and practised for so long, all his wisdom and attainments, his manifest gifts, his initiation into the Arcana; nay, even what he had learned and comprehended by means of his five outer and inner senses; and he stood as though new born from his mother, gazing around him in confusion." Jewad then meets an aged man, who conducts him into the city and shows him all its beauties, and finally introduces him into the palace of the King. " The happy Jewad had left him no 1 Malcolm, History of Persia, Vol. II, p. 281. A customary Moslem formula when surprised or startled.

eye to see, or understanding to observe, or comprehension to know, or tongue to speak. When he entered the Royal Presence and raised his eyes to look upon the beauty of the King, he saw that he who sat upon the indescribable Throne was– Himself.

The twelfth century of the Christian era gave birth to two very important Orders–the Kadiri, and the Riifai. The founder of the former, Abdul Kadr of Ghilan, besides being an eminent mystic, was a man of great learning, and numbered among his disciples his nephew Seyyid Achmet Rufa, who subsequently founded the- Riifai–better known to Europeans as the " Howhng Dervishes "–on whom he is said to have conferred the faculty of miraculously heahng the wounds which the devotees of this Order inflict upon themselves during their extraordinary religious frenzies.

In the following century the gifted mystic poet Jelalu-'d-Din, surnamed " Er Rumi," estabhshed at Konieh, the capital of the Seljoukian Sultans, the Order of the Mevlevi– the so-called " Dancing Dervishes," in connection with the Royal College of which he was the Principal. After the incorporation of that city in the Ottoman Empire this Society became exceedingly flourishing. Endowed and honoured by the Ottoman as it had previously been by the Seljoukian Sultans, and constituting as it did the University of the Empire, state dignitaries 1 The Story of Jewdd, translated by E. W. Gibb.

2 " The Roman," from his place of residence in Rom, the Eastern Empire, which retained that name for centuries after the Turkish Conquest.

were proud to call themselves its graduates, and lay members of the Mevlevi Order of Dervishes. Even Grand Viziers did not disdain to don the kulah and vestments of the Brethren of Love, and take part in their mystical gyrations.

Although, as above remarked, the Sufi principles enunciated by Bayazid Bestemi and Djouneid are professed generally by the higher grades among the Dervishes, some of the Orders hold doctrines more purely mystical, and others more purely pantheistic than the rest. Of the more purely mystical, the Nakshibendi and Khalveti Orders are the chief representatives. Abu Bekr, the first Khahf, is looked upon as the Pir, or founder of the former Order, and AH, the third Khahf, of the latter. The successful estabhshment of other communities having caused the extinction of the two original Fraternities, they had remained unrepresented, the former until the thirteenth, and the latter until the fourteenth century, when Mohammed of Nakshibend and Omer Khalvet respectively founded Orders which assumed their names. The rule observed by the Nakshibendi Dervishes is held to be in strict accordance with that instituted by Abu Bekr, and the members of this Order five in their own homes and pursue their ordinary avocations, meeting only at stated times for the performance of rehgious exercises. And though devotion does not in Turkey at the present day, as formerly, engage the attention of men of all ranks, this Order has remained one of the most numerous and popular in the Empire.

The Order of the Khalvetis, although professing to be a revival of the primitive congregation of the Khalif Ali, practise a much more rigid austerity than was compatible with the rule originally observed of remaining in the world and fulfilhng the ordinary duties of citizens. Its members undertake to live much in retirement, and to devote a great part of their time to solitary contemplation. A legend of this Order relates that, as its Pit was on one occasion leaving his cell after a prolonged period of mystical meditation, he heard a celestial voice behind him saying, "O Omer Khalvet! Why dost thou leave us? " and, accepting this as a divine injunction, he resolved to consecrate the rest of his days to such contemplation, and to institute an Order bearing his name, which signifies " Retirement."

The Order of the Bektashis which, in addition to its numerous adherents among the Osmanlis, is said to include in its ranks some 80,000 Albanian Moslems, was instituted about the same period by Hadji Bektash–" Bektash the Pilgrim "–one of the many learned men whom the munificence of the early Ottoman Princes attracted to Asia Minor from Khorassan. Orchan, who is said to have attributed many of his victories to the presence in his army of this holy man, built for him at Sivas a monastery and college, and sought his approval and blessing on every undertaking. And when the Emir had

J. B. Brown, The Dervishes.

2 The title of " Sultan " was not assumed by the earlier Ottoman rulers, who styled themselves simply " Princes."

enrolled that first fair young band of Christian boys which was destined to develop into " the strongest and fiercest instrument of imperial ambition ever devised upon earth," he led them to the abode of the saintly Sheikh, and begged of him to bestow upon them his blessing. With his arm, draped in the wide sleeve of his mantle, stretched over the head of a youth in the front rank, Hadji Bektash thus addressed the Emir:–

" The troop which thou hast now formed shall be called Yeni Sheri (New Troop). Their faces shall be white and shining, their right arms strong, their sabres keen, and their arrows sharp. They shall be fortunate in battle, and never leave the field save as dctors."

The Yeni Sheri, or Janisseries, in consequence of this benediction, remained, until the destruction of their corps in 1826, closely incorporated with the Order founded by this famous Sheikh.

The various Dervish Orders were not, it would seem, originally designated, as now, by the names of their respective founders, but by the principles they severally professed; but as each community grew in course of time more distinct from the rest, the name of the Pir was adopted to distinguish its members. The twelve communities which existed at the time of the foundation of the Ottoman Empire

Creasy, History of the Ottoman Turks, pp. 14-15. 2 Von Hammer, Histoire de IEmpire Ottomane, Vol. II, p. 71.

See below, p. 187.

have now increased to thirty-six, with as many subordinate branches.

The Kalenderi Dervishes, or " Kalenders," as they are often called by translators, are not, strictly speaking, an Order, as they are not descended from either of the original congregations. Their founder, Kalender Yussuf-Andalusi, was a native of Andalusia, and for long a disciple of Sheikh Hadji Bektash, from whose brotherhood he was finally expelled on account of his overbearing temper, and arrogant behaviour. He then made unsuccessful attempts to gain admittance to the Mevlevi Order, and ended by estabhshing on his own authority a Brotherhood the rules of which included the obligation of perpetual wandering, and of entertaining an eternal hatred against the Orders from which he had been excluded. The title of Kalender, which he assumed and bestowed on his followers, signifies " pure," implying the purity of heart, spirituality of soul, and exemption from worldly contamination which Yussuf required in his disciples–qualities somewhat at variance, one might suppose, with the above-mentioned obligation. This same title of Kalendery it may be remarked, is also given to Dervishes of all Orders who are distinguished among their brethren for superior spirituality. It is this class of " enhghtened" beings which has produced so many dangerous fanatics in every age of Mohammedanism. From it have come the assassins of Sultans, Viziers, and Grandees of the Empire, and all the unconscious imposters who, under the title of Mahdi, have misled thousands and desolated whole countries by their supposed prophecies and divine revelations.

The attainment of a high degree of sanctity being thus the aim of every true Dervish, he seeks, in order to attain this, to lead a hfe of sinless retirement from the world, and spends his days and nights in prayer and meditation. Fully impressed with the possibility of ultimately attaining intimate divine communion, the aspirant after it looks upon every mundane interest as unworthy of consideration; his mind becomes more and more completely absorbed in mystic contemplation; and as the result of his constant invocation of the name of the Deity, he hears, even when in the midst of a noisy crowd, no other sound but Allah! Allah! unless, indeed, it be some divine command addressed to him in return. The more destitute a Dervish is of worldly goods, the fewer are his ties to earth; the more emaciated his body with privation and fasting, the greater his advance in spirituality; the ills of existence affect him not, and death has for him no terrors. His solitude is cheered by the presence of angelic visitors who impart to him wondrous things hidden from the ken of ordinary mortals. Or they are the bearers of direct messages from the Deity, who thus makes known to his servants His holy Will concerning men; and when commanded to do so, the Dervish fearlessly denounces, in the name of Allah, the great ones of the earth who, by their misdeeds, have incurred the divine displeasure.

3–(2119)

CHAPTER II

THE SPIRITUAL HIERARCHY

" A Saint is aware of every thought of the King's heart, and of every secret on earth or in heaven."– Saying of Jelalu-'d-Din.

It is noteworthy that Mohammed, in proclaiming himself to be the Messenger of Allah, connected himself with the past as the Last of the Prophets. The Moslem hierarchy of inspired Seers begins with Adam, and includes the patriarchs Noah and Abraham as well as the greater Jewish Prophets and Christ, each successive one being esteemed greater than his predecessor. But in addition to this historical hierarchy of Prophets there exists, in Moslem belief, another of an entirely mythical character– a succession of saintly beings unto whom the Will of Allah has been revealed, and through whose instrumentality the destinies of mankind are governed. Supreme among these Saints of the Moslem Calendar is Khizr, or Khidhr-Elias, a mythical personage who from time immemorial has in various forms and under different names, filled a prominent place in the religions of the world. This protean Saint, or Demi-god, appears to be identifiable with the Prophet Elijah, or Elias, as well as with the Christian St. George, who, in his turn, has been identified with Horus. Khidhr is held to have

Comp. Lenormant, Origines ii, p. 12; Clermont-Ganneau, Rev. Arch, xxx, pp. 388-397; Guyard, Rev. de VHistoire des Religions, 1880, p. 344; Gaston Paris, Acad, des Inscriptions, etc., 1880, pp. 91-116.

had his original abode in the terrestrial Paradise which contained a tree of Life and a Fountain of Life; and having eaten of the fruit of the one and drunk of the water of the other he became immortal. As the wisest of created beings, he was consulted by

Moses, who, accompanied by Joshua, journeyed to a place where two rivers met, or, according to other writers, to an " Isle of the Isles of the sea," where they found the Sage from whom Moses received the secret of the " True Path." Another legend gives the following account of this journey:–

" The prophet of Israel, in one of his interviews with Allah on Mount Sinai, prayed for wisdom to comprehend the hidden mysteries. That is too hard a matter for thee, replied the Almighty. But on the Prophet's insisting, He relented and said, Make then for thyself iron shoes and get ready a cooked fish. Then set out. Thou wilt walk until the shoes are worn out and the fish has returned to hfe, and then wilt thou find the man who shall instruct thee in the knowledge of mysteries.

" Moses did as the Lord bade him, and, accompanied by St. John the Baptist, he set out. In the evening Moses and John ate some of the fish, yet the next day they found it again whole. After a long 1 This " Water," " Fountain," " Stream," or " River of Life," said to exist in a Land of Darkness in the extreme East, is an Oriental myth alluded to in Revelations xxii. 1, and often made use of by Ottoman and Persian poets. It frequently occurs also in the folk-tales of South-Eastern Europe.

2 See p. 104.

journey they arrived at a spot where two seas met. Moses lay down to sleep, and John was watching over him, when suddenly a drop of spray fell on the fish, which immediately came to life again and plunged into the sea. When Moses awoke he set out again with John, who had told him nothing of the resuscitated fish. Towards evening they stopped to eat, but the fish was not there. St. John then revealed what he had seen, and Moses returned to the place where the fish had leapt into the sea. There they found a man l3nng on the ground. Moses saluted him respectfully, and the prostrate man returned his salute, sa3dng, Health to thee, Moses, my father.

" Who told thee that I am Moses?

" Allah, who has sent me to thee.

This man was Khidhr. What wilt thou with me? he asked.

" I will that thou instruct me in the knowledge of mysteries. I will follow thee wherever thou goest.

" Thou canst not follow me, said Khidhr, nor art thou able to acquire the knowledge of mysteries.

" I will follow thee, and I will strive to learn of thee.

" Thou mayest follow me on one condition only–that thou meddle not in my business.

" Moses accepted the condition. Then, sending back John the Baptist to his own country, Moses and Khidhr asked for passage on board a ship which was about to set sail. The two men had no money, and their clothes were ragged. The captain at first refused to take them on board, but finally yielded to their sohcitations, and allowed them to sail with him.

" After a long voyage they arrived in a port; but before going ashore Khidhr made a great hole in the vessel in which he had had a free passage.

" What injustice! what wickedness! thought Moses to himself.

Khidhr, who reads the hearts of men, remarked to him, Said I not to thee that the knowledge of mysteries is difficult to acquire, and hast thou not promised to meddle not in my affairs?

" Moses held his peace.

" As they passed through a town, Khidhr perceived in a lonely spot a beautiful child asleep, and cut off its head. The soul of Moses revolted against this crime, but he said nothing. They left the town, and came to the country. Seeing a wall about to fall in ruins, Khidhr straightened it, and, with the help of Moses, left it in good repair.

" What folly, thought Moses to himself, Khidhr kills an innocent child, and then repairs an old ruined wall in the fields!

" Khidhr was aware of the reflections of Moses. You find unjust, he said, the deeds I have done in your company; you are blaming me. I will explain to thee the motives of my conduct: Listen! I scuttled the vessel in which we had a free passage. It belongs to five persons of whom three are orphans under age whose sole Uvehhood is the profit they derive from it. In the city where we landed is a tyrant who seizes upon every sound vessel which enters the port. The vessel which brought us, being unsound, he has let go on her way.

I cut off the head of the sleeping child because, had he grown up, he would have been the cause of great misfortunes to his country and to its religion.

" We mended the ruined wall, and that seemed to thee labour thrown away. This wall belongs to some young children, and conceals a hidden treasure. Had it fallen down, the first passer-by would have found this treasure; it will now stand firm till the children are grown up, and they will enjoy their own.

" I told thee that thou wert not able to follow me, or to acquire the knowledge of mysteries. Said I not truly? Go thou on thy way.

" And Khidhr disappeared."

Khidhr is also credited in Moslem behef with having led the Israelites out of Egypt and guided them through the Red Sea and the Desert, taking the place of the " pillars of cloud and of fire " in the Biblical account of this incident. Moslems also hold that Khidhr-EHas, as he is often termed, though really one single individual, has a dual personality. He is regarded as the special protector of travellers, being invoked under the former name by those journejdng on the sea, and under the latter by those journeying on land. Both parts of this dual personage are believed to be perpetually wandering over the world, Khidhr on the sea, and Elias on the land, and to meet once a year at Mina, near Mekka, on the day of the " Station of the Pilgrims." He is thus connected with St. Nicholas, who performs the same good offices for the Greeks, and is the special patron of sailors. St. Nicholas is also further confounded with HXto?, with Ah, the nephew of the Prophet, and with Phineas, the immortal hero of Talmudic legend who is credited with the performance of twelve miracles, and, according to that authority, destined, hke Ehas, to play an important part at the end of the world. This behef would appear to be illustrated in the question addressed to Jesus by his disciples: Why say the Scribes that Ehas must first come? " and in His answer that " Ehas is come already and they knew him not," 2 as also in the popular Eastern behef in the periodic incarnation of this mythical being.

Numerous instances are recorded in Moslem literature and legend of the sudden appearances and disappearances of Khidhr-Elias. By many he is held to be always visibly present somewhere on the earth, and like his prototype the Tishbite, is often " carried by the Spirit of the Lord " from place to place. Could he be recognised, a knowledge of the secret of immortality might be demanded of him; but it is only a saintly man who can distinguish Khidhr from another. A Moslem desirous of an 1 A Greek couplet says of this Saint:–

He to our aid comes on the sea, And on the land works wondrously.

2 Matt. xvii. 10, 12.

interview with this mysterious being, must, according to Turkish popular behef, perform his devotions during forty consecutive days under the central dome of the mosque of St. Sofia at Constantinople, and on the fortieth day he is certain to be rewarded with a sight of Khidhr-Ehas. Evliya Effendi, "The Traveller," himself a member of a distinguished Dervish family, declares in his Narrative that " thousands of holy men have here enjoyed the happiness of converse with that great Prophet." And many are the quaint and fantastic legends current in the Turkish capital concerning interviews with this Master of Secrets." 2

One of these legends relates that a pious Turk who had undertaken the quest of Khidhr, met, on the fortieth day, in the vicinity of the mosque, a stranger, who said to him, "The mosque is not yet open; Why comest thou to disturb the sleep of its guardians?"

" I come to seek Khidhr," he rephed.

" Dost thou know him?"

" I know him not."

" Then follow me, and I will show him to thee."

Khidhr–for it was indeed he whom the True Behever had met–went on before him, and the pious man observed that his feet left an imprint on the stones over which he walked.

Narrative of Travels, p. 60.

2 One of these, more marvellous even than the following, is given by Evliya Effendi, who concludes it with the remark–" The proof rests with the relater." Part I, pp. 60-63.

" Dost thou know what Khidhr can do? " asked the stranger.

No," rephed the pious man.

Khidhr can thrust his finger into stone even as I do."

His finger entered the stone as he spoke, and the stone " perspired " abundantly.

" When thou seest a man who does wonders such as these, say to thyself, This is Khidhr! and hold him fast."

" I will not fail," he rephed, and his companion disappeared.

The pious man entered the mosque and related his adventure to its guardians.

" Twas Khidhr himself! " they cried. " If thou see him again, fail not to hold him fast, and let him go only when he has fulfilled thy desire."

The man performed his devotions in the mosque for another forty days, and on the morning of the fortieth he met a stranger who accosted him as the other had done.

I would see Khidhr," he again rephed.

" What seekest thou from him? " asked the stranger.

Then the pious man concluded that this was indeed Khidhr, and he seized and held him fast.

" I am not Khidhr," said the stranger.

1 Stones into which Khidhr is beheved to have thrust his finger are held to cure those afflicted with profuse perspiration. The sufferer inserts his finger into the cavity, strokes with it his forehead and eyehds, and, it is confidently asserted, " goes away cured."

" Yea, thou art he!"

" I am not. Suffer me to go on my way, and I will show thee Khidhr."

" Yea, thou art indeed Khidhr," insisted the pious man. " Fulfil my desire, or I will proclaim aloud who thou art and others will then hkewise seize and hold thee."

I tell thee again I am not he whom thou seekest. Thou wilt see Khidhr on Friday in the mosque at the hour of the noontide namaz. He who shall place himself on thy right hand at the moment the pubhc prayers begin will be Khidhr; hold him fast." So saying, the stranger disappeared.

Friday came, and the True Believer repaired to the mosque of St. Sofia for the noontide prayer. Just as the service was beginning, a man, dressed as an Usher of the Subhme Porte, placed himself on his right. As they came out of the mosque the pious man seized the Usher, sa5ang,

" Thou art Khidhr! I will not let thee go!"

The Usher stoutly denied that he was other than his dress betokened him, and did his best to get away from the pious man. A long struggle ensued. The two men wrestled, fell, and rose again, until they came to the cemetery outside the Adrianople gate of the city. The window of a turhe stood open, and the usher chmbed through it, closely followed by the pious man, who still held on to his clothing, and after various turns, they came into a splendid

The mausoleum erected over the tomb of a reputed saint. Many famous Dervishes are buried in this cemetery.

Ia.

A WANDERING DERVISH subterranean hall. Round it were ranged forty sheep-skin mats, thirty-eight of which were occupied by venerable-looking men. The stranger was the chief of the Forty, one of whom had just died, and the pious man was allowed to take his place.

" Thou mayst seat thee on any mat thou wilt save that which is reserved to me, said the Usher, who was the Sheikh of the Forty, as he and his companions prepared to go out on the morrow.

The pious man obeyed, and remained in the underground dwclhng for cight days, during which he was left alone from morning until sunset. But on the eighth day the True Beuever, moved by curiosity, seated himself on the sheepskin of the Chief. Suddenly he saw as in one glance the whole world with everything in and upon it, even to the innermost thoughts of men, and was filled with wonder and dehght. As the hour for the return of the thirty-nine approached, he took another seat, where they found him.

" What hast thou done? " they demanded in voices of thunder.

" I have done naught."

" Yea, thou didst sit in the forbidden seat."

" Nay, I did not," mendaciously rephed the pious man.

But scarcely had he said the words than the hall became dark, and he found himself again in the cemetery outside the Adrianople gate.

An anecdote recorded by Eflaki as a proof of the 1 Acts of the Adepts, Redhouse's Mesnevi, p. 78.

exceptional spiritual gifts of Jelalii-'d-Din also illustrates the same belief regarding Khidhr, When this great Dervish poet was still quite young, he was one day preaching on the subject of Moses and EHas. During the discourse one of his disciples noticed a stranger seated in a comer pa5dng great attention, and every now and then exclaiming, "Good! " " Quite true! " " " Quite correct! " " " He might have been the Third with Us Two! " etc. It occurred to the disciple that this might be Khidhr-Ehas. He therefore grasped his garment, and begged for his spiritual aid.

" Oh! " said the stranger, " seek aid rather from your master, as we all do. Every mystic saint of Allah is the loving and admiring friend of Jelal."

So saying, he disengaged his robe from the disciple's grasp, and instantly vanished.

The Murtd then went to pay his respects to his master, who at once addressed him with the words, "Ehas and Moses and the Prophets are all friends of mine. The Dervish understood the allusion, and became thereafter a still more ardent follower of his Sheikh.

According to the mystical canon, there are always on earth a certain number of holy men who are admitted to intimate communion with the Deity. The one who occupies the highest position among his contemporaries is called the " Axis " (Qutb) or " Pole " of his time. As EUas was in his day an " Axis," and indeed as such held a higher spiritual 1 Koran, Chap, xviii. 59-81.

rank than all other Qutbs, it is his privilege to appoint his successors in office. This prevalent behef accords curiously with the bibhcal story of his investiture of Ehsha with his own miraculous powers and offices, and of the subjection of all contemporary Prophets to both in turn, and forms a strong hnk in the chain with which the Dervishes connect their doctrines and powers with those of the Prophets, Seers, and Patriarchs of old. These " Poles" are quite unrecognisable as such, save by other holy men, and may belong to any rank in hfe, as is illustrated in the following story told by Evhya Effendi.

When the terrible conqueror, Timour the Tartar, was marching against Broussa, the alarmed inhabitants asked the eminent Dervish, Emir Sultan, who resided there, what would be the fate of their city. The Sheikh rephed that, as Broussa was under the special protection of Khidhr and of Eskedji Hodja, these holy men must be informed of the approach of the enemy. He accordingly sent a letter by the hand of one of his Dervishes to Eskedji Hodja, who was found in the Tartar camp. When the Saint, who was busy mending a torn garment, had read the missive, he stuck his needle into his turban, exclaiming, "Emir Sultan shall be obeyed! " and before he had finished putting his work into his bag, the camp was, at his unuttered 1 Complimentary titles of " Pasha," "Emir," or " Sultan " were frequently bestowed on learned men in the palmy days of the Ottoman Empire. See pp. 61 and 167.

2 Literally " The Patching-tailor Parson."

command, broken up. " For, adds the narrator, " this old tailor was a Qutbj a Pole of Poles, and a Chief among Saints."

Subordinate to the Qtltb are two holy beings who bear the title of The Faithful Ones," and are assigned places on his right and left respectively. Below these is a quartette of " Intermediate Ones " Evtdd); and on successively lower planes are five " Lights" (Envdr), and seven " Very Good" (Akhydr). The next rank is filled by forty Absent Ones" (Rijal-i-ghaib), also termed Martyrs" (Shuheda). When an " Axis" quits this earthly existence, he is succeeded by the " Faithful One " who has occupied the place at his right hand, and the vacancies thus caused are filled up from the successive ranks.

" The Absent Ones " are said to have a circular plan, or map, of the world, having for its centre the holy city of Mekka. It is divided into thirty sections corresponding with the days of the Mohammedan month, and on it are also denoted the points of the compass. The Forty set out from Mekka every morning in the direction indicated by their map for that day, returning before the end of twenty-four hours to make their report to the " Axis." Any one possessing a copy of their map can, by consulting it, ascertain where the " Absent Ones " may be found at a given time, and by placing himself in their path may obtain from them whatever spiritual boon he may desire. For to these holy men, who also bear the collective titles of " Lords of Souls," and " Directors, is committed a spiritual supremacy over mankind far exceeding the temporal authority of earthly rulers. The transactions and designs of every individual are believed to be under their control, and must receive their approval, or at least permission, before they can be carried into effect. For they are the Deputies of the Prophets and Saints who have left the world, and to them is divulged the will of Allah with regard to the actions of men.

According to Mr. Lane's account of these mystical beings the Axis' is, Hke Khidhr, " often seen, but not recognised as such; and the same is said of all who hold authority under him. He always has a humble demeanour and mean dress, and mildly reproves those whom he finds acting impiously, particularly those who have a false reputation for sanctity. Though he is unknown to the world, his favourite stations are well known, yet at these places he is seldom visible. It is asserted that he is almost constantly seated on the roof of the Kaabah; and though never seen there, is always heard at midnight to cry twice, O Thou most merciful of those

Sadi thus refers in his Gulistan to these mystical beings. (I quote from Mr. Davis's translation.)

A group of Directors, in lonely retreat,
With their breath full of fire, although earthly their feet–
They root up a hill from its site, with a cry;
And a kingdom demolish at once, with a sigh.
Like the wind theyre unseen, and of hurricane speed;
Like stones they are silent, and rosaries read.

The Modern Egyptians, who show mercy! which cry is then repeated by the Moeddins from the minarets of the temple; but a respectable pilgrim, whom I have just questioned upon this matter, has confessed to me that he himself has witnessed that this cry is made by a regular minister of the mosque, yet that few pilgrims know this: he believes, however, that the roof of the Kaabah is the chief station of the Axis. Another favourite resort of this revered and unknown person is the gate of Cairo. Though he has a number of favourite stations, he does not abide solely at these, but, hke Khidhr, wanders through the world, among persons of every rehgion, whose appearance, dress, and language he assumes; and distributes to mankind, chiefly through the agency of the subordinate Welees, the evils and blessings apportioned to each by his Kismet.

Mr. J. P. Brown also describes an encounter which a Dervish friend of his had with one of these " Lords of Souls," or, as he terms them, "Spiritual Owners," while on a pilgrimage to the tomb of the Khahf Ah. His name was Jemel-ed-Din of Kufa, and the Dervish described him as a person of middle stature, perfectly naked, with scanty hair and beard, of feeble frame, and apparently some forty to fifty years of age. When the Dervish came up with him in the desert and ahghted from his horse for the purpose of offering his homage, the saint turned round suddenly, and cried in a loud voice, "Go to Allah 1 " The pilgrim was too startled and frightened to kiss the hand of the holy man as he had intended, and returned to Kufa, which place he had passed on his way. On enquiring at the mosque there for the abode of this Saint, he was shown a spot near the tomb of the Khahf Ah's nephew, where he was said to sleep on a mat of date-palm leaves, with a stem for his pillow. The Dervish asked how he was supported, and in what way he passed his time; but could obtain no further information about him, save that he came there every night to sleep, and left again in the morning for the desert. This person, it appears, died in 1882 (A. H. 1260,) and has been succeeded in his saintly rank by an individual of the name of Beder ed Din, who will Hve till 1902 (A. H. 1280) when the " Last of the Saints " will take his place.

Below the " Absent Ones " is another class of saints called Abddls, from among whom the higher ranks are recruited as vacancies occur. These persons would, I fear, in more highly civihsed countries be termed idiots or lunatics. Orientals, however, treat with reverence what they cannot explain; and, according to the popular behef, the Abddls are beings so holy that their souls have already found their way to heaven, and their bodies are consequently left on earth without the guidance of ordinary reason. As none but Allah knows who has in reahty been promoted to fill the place of a defunct " Absent One," any Abddl may be credited with that honour. The result of this reputation 1 The Dervishes.

4-(2119) for sanctity enjoyed by Ahddls is that they are allowed to wander at large over the country, sometimes half clad, sometimes completely naked, following the bent of their errant fancies; and the wilder and more extraordinary their vagaries, the greater is their renown for virtue and hohness. They are no respecters of persons, but denounce with impunity high and low, pasha or peasant, who may chance to incur their anger or dislike; and though the more enhghtened portion of the pubhc may estimate these maniacs at their just value, they will at the same time avoid any couision with them, as their abusive threats when excited are attributed by the ignorant to divine inspiration.

Many of those, however, who are termed Ahddls, or Perishdns, are in full enjoyment of all their faculties, but, possessed by an aversion for their fellow-men, shun their abodes, and, like the hermits of Christendom, retire to mountains and deserts where, fed perhaps on ' locusts and wild honey "–though the popular behef credits them with the faculty of being able to dispense altogether with food–they live in harmony with wild animals whose fierceness or timidity they overcome by means of their wonderful spiritual powers.

A succession of famous Ahddls has existed in Turkey extending from the time of the conquest to the present day, and the renown of many has been so great that we find their sayings and doings chronicled by the historians and writers of their times. During the reign of Sultan Orchan, the most famous were Abddl Mousa and Abddl Murad, who were with the army at the conquest of Broussa, and whose tombs in that city are still visited by devout pilgrims. The " Sultan of all Saint-fools," commonly called Sabah-Sabah, was, according to Evhya Effendi, the son of a sergeant of the Jani-series, and hved in the reign of Mohammed IV. Having foretold his father's death on the day before it took place, the word Sabah (to-morrow) was retained by him as his nickname. During the Grand Vizierate of Kara Mustapha, he one day made a great disturbance at the Divan by clamouring for the hberation of his mother, who had been imprisoned for smoking tobacco, a practice, it would appear, not then permitted to women. " Release," he cried, " the women, and imprison the men if you will, for I have no father." " Thus," adds the narrator, he got his mother released."

Among the many Saints and other Dervishes who accompanied the army of Mohammed III in his campaign into Hungary, was an individual who held a Colonel's commission. When the war was over he was speechless for seven years, and then was only heard to repeat the words Yetmish grush (seventy piastres), by which name he was thereafter called. He, however, subsequently prophesied to Sultan Murad IV that he would take Erivan and lose it again within seven days. This Sultan was known to assert that, though "Yetmish grush

Narrative of Travel.

had remained behind in Constantinople, he perpetually heard in the camp the prophetic words of the Ahddl. This saintly personage affected the dress of a soldier of the Bosnian frontier, and possessed the strange faculty of walking about the muddy streets of the capital without soiling even the soles of his babouches–a miraculous feat, indeed, if the state of the streets in wet weather was then anything like what it is at the present day.

Another famous Abddl of those times, Durmich D6d6h, frequented the Castle of Rumili, at the entrance of the Bosphorus, and sailors were in the habit of propitiating him on their arrival in port with an oka (about 2- lbs.) of meat. He advised ship captains concerning the voyages they were about to make. If they followed his counsel, it turned to their advantage; but if they disregarded it, ill luck was sure to accompany them. Those who passed him on their way to the Divan were also forewarned, by his behaviour towards them, whether they were or were not likely to prosper that day in their suits at law.

That this canonisation of persons of weak intellect still continues, will be seen from the following story, as related to Lady Blunt and myself by Sheikh Ah, a Bektashi of Salonica. I give, as nearly as possible, a literal translation of his own words:–

My younger brother had been, from his childhood, of an erratic and unmanageable disposition. It was impossible to teach him anything, and he

Narrative of Travel.

spent the greater part of his time in roaming from village to village, fed by the charitable, but housed I know not how, and occasionally returning home to me for a few days. As he grew older, he became confirmed in these wandering habits, and was seldom at home. He returned one day from a prolonged excursion complaining that he felt unwell, and asked to be allowed to he down in my room. He was very thirsty and feverish, and ere long smallpox declared itself. The elders of the Tekkeh, at my request, came in and prayed over him. When they had finished, he smiled, thanked them, and requested that they would come again in four days time, at the same hour, for on that day, at noon, he would die. The Dervishes, deeply affected, promised to do as he wished, and withdrew. For the next three days he was unconscious, his sight failed, and I saw that his case was hopeless. On the fourth day, at the hour he had mentioned, he came to himself, and asked me to send for the Brethren. I did so, and they again prayed over him. Then, turning to me, he said, My brother, I have been a sore burden to you all my hfe. I pray you, make me heldl (free gift) of all the bread I have eaten at your hands, so that I may depart in peace. I made the heldl, holding the poor saint's head on my knees. He then said, I am content, and breathed his last 1 One of the ceremonies at a Moslem funeral is the giving of heldl by the friends and relatives of the defunct. It conveys pardon for any offence committed towards them, and is the Moslem equivalent for the Christian requiescat in pace.

just as the clock struck the hour of noon. My community pronounced him an evliya (saint) and he was buried with the honour due to one who had held communion with Allah."

Patron saints also hold no unimportant place in this mystical hierarchy. They include, besides defunct Dervishes of peculiar holiness, all the more famous bibhcal characters; and their protection is perhaps specially claimed by the numerous eswas or trade guilds. Thus the Bakers, who, according to Evliya Effendi, have precedence over all other guilds of handicraftsmen, and enjoy the honourable title of " Columns of Faith," have for their patron Adeim, who, say the Moslems, was forbidden to eat of the corn-tree in Paradise, but having transgressed the divine command, he was exiled to earth, where Gabriel brought again to him the corn, which he boiled and converted into soup. Hence the form of invitation usual now in the East: " Come, let us eat the Father's soup (ash haha) together! " Gabriel then taught Adam to grind the corn and make it into bread.

The mythical Jemshid, who is reputed to have lived a thousand years and to have invented three hundred arts, protects, among others, the Firework-makers. The patron saint of the Coffee-makers is 1 This plural form of the Arabic word is popularly used as a singular noun, 2 Jemshid was the fourth king of the first Persian dynasty mentioned in the Shah Nameh, where he is described as having been eminent in learning and wisdom. When he

Ebul Hassan Schaseli, who discovered the virtues of the Mocha berry; that of the Gardeners is Baba Reten, a recluse of Mount Olympus, learned in botany; and that of the Dentists, or rather barber tooth-drawers, Sheikh Uwais, mentioned in the preceding chapter.

had reached the summit of his power and glory, he was able to compel the very demons to labour for him in building a glorious palace.

He taught the unholy demon train to knead Water and clay, with which, formed into bricks, The walls were built, and then high turrets, towers, And balconies, and roofs to keep out rain And cold and sunshine. Every art was known To Jemshid, without rival in the world.

CHAPTER III

THE METAPHORS OF THE POETS

" The Mystic Word, clad in poetic dress, The shadow is of that proclaimed by Prophet tongue; Majestic strideth Prophecy in foremost rank, While follows humbly in its footsteps Poesy."

One of the chief peculiarities of Persian and Ottoman poetical writings is that they almost always contain, concealed beneath their literal meaning, an esoteric and spiritual signification. A certain number of famous poems, such as, for instance, the Turkish 'Diwdn of Ashik Pasha," and the Persian " Mesnevi of Jelalii-d-Din, may, indeed, be read for the most part for what they appear on the surface to be– religious or moral works. But nearly all the long Persian romances in verse called Mesnevi, the charming love-stories of Leyla and Mejnoun, of Khusruf and Shir in, of Yusuf and Zulaikha, the Mantic Uttair, and many others, are allegorical representations of the yearning of the soul of man for union with the Deity, or its love of and quest for the highest type of spiritual beauty and goodness– an object attained only when the heart has been purified by the severest and most painful trials.

The Ghazels, or odes, present the same characteristic as the longer poems. Though on the surface either mere bacchanalian verses or voluptuous love songs, they are, to those who possess the key to their symbohc imagery, the fervent outpourings of hearts ecstasied, or, as they express it, intoxicated

THE METAPHORS OF THE POETS 45 with spiritual love. For every word in these effusions has its mystical signification. It has indeed been asserted that " every word of Sadi possesses seventy-two different meanings; and the symbolism of his verse he himself thus explains:–

Think not, O Khjzr, thou favoured of Fortune,

When I of " Wine " sing, the juice of the grape I am praising. " Wine " is to me that which bove self exalteth; None other ever doth gladden my banquet. Know that my "Cupbeajrer " is but of vow the fulfilment; " Draught " from the " Tavern " ecstatic oblivion. Heaven is my witness that long as on earth I have sojourned. Neer hath the tip of my lips with the red wine been stainm.

The " Fair One " for whom in these ghazels Man, the " Lover sighs, is the Deity; as is also the " Loved One whom he entreats to throw off the veil that conceals His perfect beauty from view. The " Ruby Lip " signifies the unspoken, but heard and understood, words of God; " nestling in the Fair One's tresses " denotes comprehension of the hidden attributes of the Divinity; the " Embrace " is the revelation to man of the divine mysteries; " Separation " or " Absence " from the " Loved One " is the non-attainment of oneness with the Deity. " Wine " is the Divine Love; the " Cupbearer " the spiritual instructor, the " giver of the goblet of celestial aspiration "; the " Libertine " the Saint who has become careless of human conventionalities; the " Tavern," a place where one mortifies sensuality, and relinquishes his name and worldly fame. The " Zephyr " is the breathmg of the Divine Spirit; the " Taper," the heavenly light kindling the "

Torch," which is the heart of the Lover, Man; and so on through every detail. These ghazels breathe, indeed, in every line a spirit of ravishment and ecstasy, picturing the whole creation as filled with the Divine Love by which even the most humble plant is excited to seek the subhme object of its desires."

One of the earhest and most famous of the Dervish poets was Mohammed ben Ibrahim of Nischapiir, on whom was conferred the honorific title of Farid-'d-Din (" Pearl of the Faith "), and who was also known by the soubriquet of " Attar " from his trade as a perfumer. He was born in 1119, and at the advanced age of a hundred and ten was massacred by the Mongols under Yenghiz Khan. One day, when he was in his shop, a passing Dervish stopped before him, cast a glance over his wares, and heaved a deep sigh. Attar, surprised, begged him to go on his way. " Thou art right," rephed the stranger, " the road to eternity is easy for me; I have no encumbrances, for all I possess in the world is my mantle. Unfortunately it is not so with thee, who possessest so much valuable merchandise. But take heed that thou also prepare thyself for that journey." This advice, according to the biographers, made a great impression on Attar's mind, and finally caused him to give up his business and the world in order to consecrate himself exclusively to the service of 1 Ubicini, Letters, p. 101.

THE METAPHORS OF THE POETS 47

God. For several years he abandoned himself to physical mortifications and rehgious practices, and subsequently made the pilgrimage to Mekka. He also frequented the society of men famed for eminent piety, and by this means collected the vast store of anecdotes with which he embelhshed and illustrated his writings, these anecdotes being considered valuable fragments of Moslem biography. In his old age Attar received at Nischapiir the visit of Jelalii-'d-Din, to whom he presented a copy of his work, the " Asrdr Ndmd, or " Book of Secrets," the perusal of which was said to have greatly influenced the younger poet. The most famous of Attar's works is, however, the Mantic Uttair," or "Language of the Birds," a long poem which represents in allegorical form the Soul's Quest for the Divine Love. The Birds had hitherto lived as a Republic, but they felt the necessity of having a King, and took counsel of the Hoopoe who, as she had, according to Moslem legend, accompanied Solomon on his journey to Sheba, was supposed to be the best judge of the quahties requisite in a King. The Hoopoe proposed to them as sovereign the Slmorg, a wonderful bird whose abode was in the Caucasus, and whose excellent qualities she set forth. The birds accept Simorg as their King; but many are dismayed by the dangers of the way and the length of the journey to his abode. A company of Birds finally set out, but the greater number perish by the way of hunger, thirst, or fatigue. At length, after passing through many trials and dangers, thirty survivors only reach the goal of their journey, when they find in themselves the object of their quest–the Sintorg, a word which, in Persian, signifies thirty birds."

This consummation is thus described by the poet.
When the birds have been introduced by the
Chamberlain into the presence of the Simorg:–
They on the Throne of Nearness take their seat In glory and in majesty's high place,
The Sun of Nearness on them shed His rays,
And, mirrored in each face, these Birds of Earth

Saw the Simorg, the Bird of Heaven;
And when on Him they gazed, but Thirty Birds beheld,
Strange wonderment then fell upon their minds.
Were they still Thirty Birds? Or were they now Simorg?
They asked themselves, and yet it seemed
That they Simorg were now, and He the Thirty Birds.

Then mutely craved the meaning to be shown Of this Plurality and Unity combined; And, without words, this did Simorg reply: 'The Sun that from my majesty rays forth A mirror is. Whoso approacheth near, Therein reflected may himself behold, His body and his soul, himself complete. Since you as Thirty Birds are hither come, You in this mirror but those Birds behold. Thus in my radiance be still lost, absorbed, That you yourselves may ever find in me." The Birds were in Simorg thenceforward lost. As are the sunrays lost within the sun.

The following passage from the same work presents another aspect of the Siifi doctrines, the pantheistic conception of Creation. It is addressed by the spiritually mmded Hoopoe to the other

Birds:–

Come! of this King admire the handiwork. Though less than naught it in His eyes appears.

THE ADRIANOPLE GATE, STAMBOUL, LEADING TO THE
DERVISH CEMETERY
THE METAPHORS OF THE POETS 49
And, as His Essence all the world pervades,
Naught in Creation is, save this alone.
Upon the waters has He fixed His Throne,
This earth suspended in the starry space,

Yet what are seas and what is air? for all Is God, and but a talisman are heaven and earth

To veil Divinity. For Heaven and earth,
Did He not permeate them, were but names.
Know then, that both this visible world, and that
Which unseen is, alike are God Himself.
Naught is, save God; and all that is, is God.
And yet, alas I by how few is He seen.
Blind are men's eyes, though all resplendent shines
The world by Deity's own light illumed.
O Thou whom man perceiveth not, although
To him Thou deignest to make known Thyself;
Thou all Creation art, all we behold, but Thou.
The soul within the body lies concealed,
And Thou dost hide Thyself within the soul.
O soul in soul! Mystry in mystry hid!
Before all wert Thou, and art more than all!

Sadi was a fellow-disciple with Bah–'d-Din (father of the great poet of Konieh) of the famous Sheikh Saed- d-Din of Kashgar, who instructed him in theology and in the principles of Siifi philosophy; and in the company of this teacher he made the first of his fourteen pilgrimages to Mekka. Sadi was a great traveller. Besides his Eastern journeys in Armenia, Arabia, and India, he also visited Europe, Egypt, and Barbary. On one occasion he was captured by the Crusaders and made to work in the ditch at Tripoli. From this slavery he was rescued by a merchant of Aleppo,

See Garcin de Tassy, Mantic Uttair. 2 Mentioned on p. 148 8 Ibid.

who recognised the poet, paid his ransom, and subsequently gave him his daughter in marriage.

The last thirty years of Sadi's long and adventurous life–he lived to the great age of a hundred and sixteen–were spent at Shiraz, a town situated among charming natural scenery, and blessed with a dehcious chmate. Here he wrote the two works on which his fame chiefly rests, the Gulistdn, or " Rosary, and the Bostdn, or " Garden." The first consists of prose anecdotes interspersed with couplets, verses, and moral apologues; while the second is entirely a poetical work. The writings of

Sadi are replete with wise proverbial sayings, pious reflections, and moral precepts, but Siifi mysticism also finds a large place in them.   In Oriental fashion he thus addresses himself:–

Sadi, move thou to Resignation's shrine.

O man of God, the path of God be thine!

Hapless is he who from this Haven turns.

All doors shall spurn him who this Portal spurns.

The tolerance and goodwill to all mankind, irrespective of race or creed, so often met with among the more enlightened Siifis, formed an admirable part of Sadi's character, and found expression as follows:–

All Adam's race are members of one frame, Since all, at first, from the same essence came. When, by hard fortune is one limb opprest, The other members lose their wonted rest, If thou feel not for others' misery, A son of Adam is no name for thee.

The Mesnevi of Jelalu-'d-Din surpasses, in

Oriental estimation, all other works of the kind by

THE METAPHORS OF THE POETS 51

Moslem writers. The word Mesnevi signifies at once the verse-form–a rhymed distich of not less than twelve couplets–in which romance or epic poetry-is written, and the poem itself; and the work of the poet of Konieh is by common consent termed simply The Mesnevi, or " Poem of Poems. Like all the early Dervish hterature, it is in Persian, and consists of a number of pieces written in the form of apologues, with digressions on Sufi doctrines. The work is divided into six Books or Parts, and contains twenty-six thousand six hundred and sixty couplets. Like his forerunner, Sadi, the great founder of the Mevlevi Order preaches tolerance and large-minded-ness, as in the following charming parable which I give in Mr. Whinfield's prose translation:–

" Moses once heard a shepherd praying as follows: O God, show me where Thou art that I may become Thy servant. I will clean Thy shoes, and comb Thy hair, and sew Thy clothes, and fetch Thee milk. When Moses heard him praying in this senseless manner, he rebuked him. saying, O foohsh one,

Portions only of the Mesnevi have, so far as my now-ledge goes, as yet been translated into any European language. The late Sir James Redhouse published in Trubner's Oriental Series a volume containing translations of a number of pieces from the First Book of that work. The renderings of the late Orientalist are, however, often grotesque in their exceeding baldness; while comparison with Mr. Whinfield's literal prose translations of the same passages makes it evident that, in order to meet the exigencies of rhyme and metre, many words and phrases have been added which completely obscure the sense of the original lines.

though your father was a Moslem, you have become an infidel! God is a spirit, and needs not such gross ministrations as in your ignorance you suppose. The shepherd was abashed at the Prophet's rebuke; he tore his clothes and fled away into the desert. Then a voice from heaven was heard, saying, O Moses, wherefore hast thou driven away My servant? Thine office it is to reconcile my people with Me, not to drive them away from Me. I have given to men different usages and forms of praising and of adoring Me. I have no need of their praises, being exalted high above all such needs. I regard not the words which are spoken, but the heart that offers them."

The following poem, which forms a kind of Prologue to the Mesneviy was translated a century ago by the celebrated Orientahst, Sir Wiuiam Jones:–

SONG OF THE REED-FLUTE 2

Hear how yon reed, in sadly pleasing tales, Departed bliss and present woe bewails: "With me, from native banks untimely torn, Love-warbling youths and soft-eyed virgins mourn.

0! let the heart by fatal absence rent,

Feel what I sing, and bleed when I lament: Who roams in exile from his parent bower. Pants to return, and chides each lingering hour. My notes in circles of the grave and gay, Have hailed the rising, cheered the closing day. Each in my fond affections claimed a part, But none discerned the secret of my heart.

1 The Works, Vol. I.

a See p. 110. The Mystic Reed-flute.

THE METAPHORS OF THE POETS 53

What though my strains and sorrows slow combined, Yet ears are dull, and carnal eyes are blind. Free through each mortal form the spirits roll, But sighs avail not. Can we see the soul?"

Such notes breathed gently from yon vocal frame.

Breathed, said I? No! Twas all enlivening flame.

Tis love that fills the reed with warmth divine;

Tis love that sparkles in the rosy wine.

The plaintive wanderer from my peerless maid,

The reed has fired, and all my soul betrayed.

He gives the bane and he with balsam cures;

Afflicts, yet soothes, impassions, yet allures.

Hail, heavenly Love! true source of endless gains!

Thy balm restores me, and thy skill sustains.

O more than Galen learned, than Plato wise,

My guide, my law, my joy supreme, arise!

Love warms this frigid clay with mystic fire,
And dancing mountains leap with young desire.
Blest is the soul that swims in seas of love,
And long the life sustained by food above.
With forms imperfect can perfection dwell?
Here pause, my song; and thou, vain world, farewell!

The following charming little parable, so essentially Sufi in spirit, is already a favourite with Europeans. It is from " The Lion's Hunt ":–

A Dervish once to his Friend's door drew nigh, and knocked. "Who art thou. Faithful One?" was asked, ere 'twas unlocked. " Tis I," the Dervish cried. " Then in thou mayst not come; For at my well-dressed feast there is for raw no room," Replied the Friend. " But separation's fiery smart Can purify the crude, and cleanse from guile his heart. Since from the bonds of self thou art not yet set free, By fiery flame alone canst thou refined be." The Dervish went away. For one whole weary year Did wander, grief-consumed, his Friend no longer near.

5–U119)

Then, cleansed at length by fire till self became as naught, He turned him back again; his Friend's abode he sought, And at His door he knocked, with trembling hand and meek, Fearing some careless word his foolish lips might speak. Again then asked the Friend: " Who at my door knocks low? " He answered only, "O Belov'd, Belov'd, 'tis thou! " " Since 'tis Myself that knocks, the door stands open wide– But could two I's beneath one roof in peace abide? "

The following passage, also from the Mesnevi, refers to the Dervish Pit, Bayazid Bestemi, mentioned in the first chapter, and interestingly illustrates the Siifi doctrine of union with the Deity. When on his pilgrimage to Mekka, Bayazid visited all the " Pillars of Insight " who had their abodes in the various towns through which he had to pass. One day he had the happiness to discover the " Axis," 2 or greatest saint of the time, in the person of a venerable Dervish with whom he held the following conversation:–

" Say now, O Bayazid, to what town art thou bound,
Where will thy weary caravan its rest have found?"
" At dawn I to the holy Kaaba take my way."
" But how wilt thou the cost of that long journey pay?"
" Two hundred silver dirhems do I bear with me,
Sewn in the corner of my cloak for safety, see!
" Walk sevn times round me, Bayazid," the Sage then said.
" Greater thy gain than hadst the Kaaba's circuit made!
As for thy dirhems, liberal one, give them to me.
For now thy journey's o'er, thou thy deshe dost see.
Thy Pilgrimage is made, Eternal Life hast gained,
Heavn's purity in one brief moment hast attained.

1 Versified from Mr. Whinfield's prose translation.
2 See p. 32.
3 The Sanctuary at Mekka.

THE METAPHORS OF THE POETS 55

That which thy soul in me doth see is truly God,
For He hath chosen me to make me His abode.
Unto the Kaaba He His Grace and Favour shows,
But to my body He His Secret doth disclose.
Hath He, since He that house built, een to enter deigned?
But, save th Eternal One, none entrance here hath gained.
When Thou hast me beheld, then Allah hast thou seen.
And round about the holy Kaaba thou hast been.
Thou servest me, and Allah worshipped is, and praised;
For think not He so high above all men is raised.
Thy mind's eye open wide, and fix thou it on me
That, in a mortal, Thou the Light of God mayst see.
Once only the Belov'd My House the Kaaba named,
But me He seventy times has as His Servant claimed.
O happy Bayazid, thou hast the Kaaba found.
And now art with a thousand precious blessings crowned!"

Jelalu-'d-Din also left behind him a large collection of ghazels, or odes. This is a verse-form which may contain from three to twenty-five distichs, the two first lines rhyming with the second line of each succeeding couplet. This pecuharity of rhyme has, however, been disregarded in the following ghazelsy translated by Professor Falconer, but may be remarked in Mr. Gibb's renderings of ghazels by Ottoman poets:–

All earthly forms, where beauty dwells enshrined, That beauty borrow from the Infinite mind, Why grieve we when the faint icflections fade?– Their source and prototype are undecayed.

The form whose beauty woos the raptured eye. The strain that steeps the soul in ecstasy. When that hath vanished, and this ceased to flow. Why weep and call it death, which seems but so?

1 Alluding to a passage in the Hadis or Traditions, which says, "Heaven and earth cannot contain me, but the heart of my faithful Servant containeth me!"

Long as the gushing fount its circle fills,
Can it forget to feed its thousand rills?
Thy soul a fount is–thoughts, shapes, sounds of earth
Flow thence, as rivers from their source have birth.
See, to what precious metal is refined Ignoble dust, when linked to godlike mind;
Nor doubt when thou hast filled thy part as man,
Angel awaits thee in the mighty plan.
With starry heaven thy home–a bright abode,
Far from the spot thy mortal footsteps trode.
Nor yet at Angel shall thy being's motion
Be stayed, but onward press to Being's ocean.
There shall thy atom-drop become a sea,
Vast as a hundred deeps, wide, weltering, boundless, free,
Then boldly, son, proclaim in faith and truth.
This creed: Though forms decay, souls own a deathless youth.

Passing on to the fifteenth century, we come to J ami, who was born in the year 1414 at the town of Jam in Khorassan, from which he took his pen-name. To his real name of Abdul-rahman was added that of Nur-'d-DIn (" Light of the Faith "), and in later years his fame for learning and sanctity gained also for him that of Mevlana (" Om" Lord " or " Master "). J ami left behind him at least fifty volumes of poetry, grammar, and theology, which are still read and admired in the Eastern world. Seven of his best mystical poems are called The Seven Thrones, but the most famous of all is his Yusuf and Zulaikha, considered by European authorities to be one of the finest compositions in the Persian language. Of the follo dng passages the first and second are taken from the introductory, 1 See Preface to Rozenzweig's translation of Yusuf and Zulaikha, also his Analysis and Specimens of the Joseph and Zulaikha, 1872. Griffith, Yusuf and Zulaikha, 1882.

THE METAPHORS OF THE POETS 57 and the third from one of the concluding cantos of this poem. In this touching story of the loves of Joseph and " Potiphar's Wife " is symbohsed the yearning of the human soul for the highest moral beauty and perfection:– (I) In solitude, where Being signless dwelt. And all the Universe still dormant lay Concealed in selfishness, One Being was Exempt from " I-" or " Thou "-ness, and apart From all duality; Beauty Supreme, Unmanifest, except unto itself By its own light, yet fraught with power to charm The souls of all; concealed in the Unseen, An essence pure, unstained by aught of ill. No mirror to reflect Its loveliness, Nor comb to touch Its locks; the morning breeze Neer stirred Its tresses; no collyrium Lent lustre to Its eyes; no rosy cheeks Oershadowed by dark curls like hyacinth. Nor peach-like down were there; no dusky mole Adorned Its face; no eye had yet beheld Its image. To Itself it sang of love In wordless measures. By Itself it cast The die of love.

But Beauty cannot brook Concealment and the veil, nor patient rest Unseen and unadmired: 'twill burst all bonds, And from Its prison casement to the world Reveal Itself. See where the tulip grows In upland meadows, how in balmy spring It decks itself; and how amidst its thorns. The wild rose rends its garment, and reveals Its loveliness. Thou, too, when some rare thought Or beauteous image, or deep mystery Flashes across thy soul, canst not endure To let it pass, but hold'st it, that perchance In speech or writing thou may'st send it forth To charm the world.

Wherever Beauty dwells Such is its nature, and its heritage From Everlasting Beauty, which emerged From realms of purity to shine upon The worlds, and all the souls that dwell therein. One gleam fell from It on the Universe And on the angels, and this single ray Dazzled the angels till their senses whirled Like the revolving sky. In divers forms Each mirror showed It forth, and everywhere Its praise was chanted in new harmonies.

Each speck of matter did He constitute
A mirror, causing each one to reflect
The beauty of His visage. From the rose
Flashed forth His beauty, and the nightingale,
Beholding it, loved madly. From that Light
The candle drew the lustre which beguiles
The moth to immolation. On the sun

His Beauty shone, and straightway from the wave
The lotus reared its head. Each shining lock
Of Leyia's hair attracted Mejuun's heart
Because some ray divine reflected shone In her fair face. Twas He to Shirin's Ups
Who lent that sweetness which had power to steal
The heart from Par viz, and from Ferhad life.

His Beauty everywhere doth show itself, And through the forms of earthly beauties shines Obscured, as through a veil. He did reveal His face through Joseph's coat, and so destroyed Zuleykha's peace. Whereer thou seest a veil, Beneath that veil He hides. Whatever heart Doth yield to love, He charms it. In His love The heart hath life. Longing for Him, the soul Hath victory. That heart which feigns to love The fair ones of this world, loves Him alone. Beware! say not " He is All-Beautiful, And we His lovers." Thou art but the glass, And He the Face confronting it, which casts

" All things shall perish save His Face." Koran xxviii. 88.

THE METAPHORS OF THE POETS 59 Its image on the mirror. He alone Is manifest, and thou in truth art hid.

Pure Love, hke Beauty, coming but from Him
Reveals itself in Thee. If steadfastly
Thou canst regard, thou wilt at length perceive
He is the mirror also–He alike
The Treasure and the Casket. " I " and " Thou"
Have here no place, and are but phantasies
Vain and unreal. Silence! for this tale Is endless, and no eloquence hath power
To speak of Him. Tis best for us to love
And suffer silently, being as naught.

(II)

No heart is that which Love neer wounded; they Who know not lover's pangs are soulless clay. Turn from the world, O turn thy wandering feet; Come to the World of Love and find it sweet! Heaven's giddy round from craze of love was caught, From Love's disputes the world with strife is fraught. Love's slave be thou if thou would fain be free: Welcome love's pangs, and happy shalt thou be.

Love's sweet, soft memories youth itself restore; The tale of love gives fame for evermore. If Majuun neer the cup of love had drained, High fame in heaven and earth he neer had gained. A thousand sages, deep in wisdom's lore, Untaught of Love, died, and are known no more: Without a name or trace in death they sank, And in the book of time their name is blank.

The following dialogue occurs between Yusuf and Zulaikha on meeting after a long separation, during which her husband, the Wazir of Egypt, has died, and she has become poor and bhnd. This 1 Translated by Mr. R. T. H. Browne in A Year Among the Persians, pp. 125-7.

2 Griffith, Yusuf and Zulaikha, p. 23.

separation " of course symbolises the estrangement of the human heart from the Divine Love:–

Where are thy youth, and thy beauty, and pride'?"
" Gone, since I parted from thee," she repued.

" Where is the Ught of thine eyes? " said he.

" Drowned in blood-tears for the loss of thee."

"Why is that cypress-tree bowed and bent?"

" By absence from thee and my long lament."

" Where are thy pearls and thy silver and gold?

And the diadem bright on thy head of old?"

They who spoke of my loved one," she answered, " shed, In the praise of his beauty, rare pearls on my head.

In return for those jewels, a recompense meet, I scattered my jewels and gold at their feet.

My crown of pure gold on their foreheads I set.

And the dust that they trod made my coronet.

I gave till the stream of my treasure ran dry,

My heart is Love's storehouse, and I am I."

Not in the Persian language alone, however, has poetical utterance been given to the mystical doctrines of the Dervishes. From the first half of the fourteenth century onward this language began to be abandoned for hterary purposes by Ottomans in favour of their native Turkish. Though both the prose and verse productions in that language, previous to the end of the following century, are adjudged by critics to be for the most part somewhat rude and uncouth, one of the earhest of these Turkish writers was of such eminence that he is to this day styled the " Father of Ottoman Literature."

1 The human form is often likened to a cypress by Oriental poets, and also by the Greek popular muse.

2 Griffith, Yusuf and Zulaikha, pp. 293-4.

THE METAPHORS OF THE POETS 61

Oriental writers have always affected anonymity, and this author wrote under the takhullus, or pen-name of Aashik (" The Loving ") to which name, according to the custom of those times, was added the title of " Pasha " to denote his high rank among men of letters. Among Aashik's numerous productions is an Ode to Culture "; but he was chiefly eminent as a mystic, having been a member of the Mevlevi Order, and his principal work is a long mystical poem known as the 'Aashik Pasha Diwdniy It consists of rhymed couplets, the following translated hues from which may give some idea of the character and sentiment of the Turkish poetry of that period:–

All the Universe, one mighty sign, is shown; God hath myriads of creative acts unknown: None hath seen them, of the races djin and men, None hath news brought from that realm far off from ken. Never shall thy mind in reason reach that strand, Nor can tongue the King's name utter of that land. Since 'tis His each nothingness with life to invest, Trouble is there neer at His behest. Eighteen thousand worlds from end to end Do not with Him one atom's worth transcend.

Khiyah lived in the first half of the sixteenth century. He began hfe as a Kalender of the School of Ah Baba, but on coming to the capital he found a patron in the Grand Vizier, who introduced him to the notice of the Sultan.

1 The race of beings created, according to Moslem tradition, before Adam.

2 Translated by Mr. Gibb in his Ottoman Poems.

GHAZEL

One with Realms Eternal this my soul to make–what wouldest say? All Creation's empire's fancies to forsake–what wouldest say? Wearing to a hair my frame with bitter sighs and moans, in love, Nestling in The Fair One's tresses, to rest take–what wouldest say? Yonder goldfaced birds within the quicksilver resplendent deep: Launching forth the hawk, my striving, these to take– what wouldest say? Yonder Nine Smaragdine Bowls of Heaven to quaff at one deep draught, Yet from all ebriety's fumes free to break– what wouldest say? To an autumn leaf the Sphere hath turned Khiyali's countenance, To the Spring of Beauty, that a gift to make–what wouldest say?

Many more examples might be given, did space allow, from the mystic poetry of Sheykhi, Lami,

Yahya Bey, and other later writers. This chapter must, however, conclude with a ghazel of Sidqi, the famous Ottoman poetess of the seventeenth century, a prolific writer, whose works are full of Sufi mysticism:–

He who union with the Lord gains, more desireth not; He who looks on charms of Fair One, other sight desireth not; Pang of love is lover's solace, eagerly he seeks therefor, Joys he in it; balm or salve for yonder blight desireth not.

Gibb, Ottoman Poems.

See my Women of Turkey, Vol. II, Chap. xxiv. " Poetesses of the Rise, Decline, and Fall of the Ottoman Empire."

THE METAPHORS OF THE POETS 63

Paradise he longs'not after, nor doth aught beside regard, Bower, or garden, mead, or youth or Hilri bright desireth not. From the hand of Power Unbounded, draweth he the wine of Ufe; Aye inebriate with knowledge, learning's light desireth not. He who Allah loveth. Lord is of an empire, such that he– King of inward mysteries– Suleyman's might desireth not: Thou art Sultan of my heart, ay, soul of my soul een art Thou; Thou art soul enow, and Sidql other plight desireth not.

Gibb, Ottoman Poems.

CHAPTER IV

MONASTERIES AND SHRINES

" If your hearts be oppressed with sorrow, go seek consolation at the graves of the holy dead."– Traditional saying of Mohammed.

The monastic establishments of the Dervish Orders, called by the various names of Tekkehs, Khdnakdhsy and Zanriyehs, but more commonly by the first, and the Turhehs, or Shrines of their Saints, are, at the present day, as numerous in European as in Asiatic Turkey. In Constantinople and its environs many of the Orders possess several establishments; and every town contains the monastery and shrine of one or more of their communities. The Tekkehs occupy for the most part picturesque and commanding situations, sometimes in the middle of towns or cities, but more frequently in their suburbs. Those of the Mevlevi and Rufai are perhaps the most remarkable. The central edifice of the former is the Sem a Khaneh (" The Hall of Celestial Sounds "), where the Brotherhood meet for the performance of their religious exercises and pubhc worship. This is usually a square building of whitewashed masonry, with a domed and red-tiled roof. The interior arrangements vary somewhat, but are always marked by the utmost simphcity. A circular space in the centre is smoothly planked and reserved for the performances of the Dervishes. It is divided by a low wooden railing from the rest of the floor, which is covered with matting and occupied during the public services by the male spectators. A gallery, supported on wooden pillars, runs round three sides of the Tekkeh; one side of it is occupied by the Mutrib, or orchestra, and the other two by the women and children, who are concealed from view by carved lattices. In some Tekkehs, where the gallery is only large enough to accommodate the orchestra, a corner of the ground floor is partitioned off for the women. The only attempts at decoration are tablets on the walls inscribed with texts from the Koran, and with the names of Allah, Mohammed, Ah, and Hasan and Husein, the grandsons of the Prophet. As in the pubhc mosques, the direction of Mekka is indicated by a niche in the wall, surmounted by the name of the Pir, or Founder of the Order, and sometimes also by the Moslem profession of faith– La ilaha il Allah ve Mohammed resoul Allah (" There is no god but Allah and Mohammed is the Prophet of Allah "), or the word Bismillah ("In the Name of Allah "). In a corner of many Tekkehs is the shrine of a departed saintly sheikh, covered with costly carpets and rich draperies, the pious offerings of those who have there sought and found healing benefit, or other boon.

The Tekkehs of the Mevlevi Order contain another apartment called the Ismi Jeleeh Hujreh, where the Brethren perform their daily namdz and the obhga-tory zikr, or calhng upon the name of Allah, which takes place at the hour of the third namdz. The courtyard surrounding the Tekkeh gives access to the cells of the monastic Dervishes and their Sheikh. These are, in a fully-equipped monastery, eighteen in number, and form a quadrangle of low buildings, with a roof sloping to the front, and covering a broad verandah into which all the doors and windows open. Beyond are flower and fruit gardens, shaded by cypress, mulberry, and plane trees, the haunts of storks and pigeons; and, enclosed by the arched gateway and tile-topped walls, are cisterns and fountains of sparkhng water furnished with iron ladles for the use of the thirsty. Sometimes, as within the precincts of the Tekkeh outside the Vardar gate of Salonica, there are also cool, shady cloisters and raised terraces and kiosks, commanding magnificent views of mountain, plain, and sea. And here, when the evening shadows are lengthening, the mystics, in their picturesque and symbolic attire, may be seen pacing tranquilly to and fro; or, seated on the broad wooden benches, meditatively passing through their fingers the brown beads of their long teshehs, or rosaries, on their faces that expression of perfect repose which indifference to the world and its doings alone can give.

Though all the Dervish Orders, in accordance with their principle of Poverty, are considered mendicant, few are so in reality, for most Tekkehs possess vakouf, or landed property bequeathed to them by pious persons. The revenues from these endowments are applied chiefly to the support of the monastic Dervishes, though the wants of a needy lay brother may occasionally be relieved from them. The Tekkehs vary greatly in point of wealth, and the more prosperous are expected to assist others less largely endowed. The Mevlevi Order is the most popular, one might even say the most fashionable, of all, and has, ever since its foundation, included among its members men of high rank. The late Sultan Abdul Aziz was, for instance, a lay Brother, and occasionally, it is said, took part in the rehgious exercises at one of the Mevlevi Tekkehs in Constantinople. This Order is, consequently, very prosperous, and its monasteries and shrines surpass those of all other Orders. The Monastery of its General, at Konieh (Iconium), in Asia Minor, possesses considerable lands bequeathed as vakouf by the old Seljukian Sultans, these bequests being ratified by subsequent princes. Murad IV, too, when marching against Persia in 1634, bestowed many favours and distinctions upon the " Sheikh of Sheikhs," as their Grand Master is termed, and endowed his community as a perpetual vakouf with the proceeds of the kharatch, the poll-tax imposed on the non-Moslem inhabitants of the city in lieu of mihtary service, now abohshed.

Notwithstanding, however, these substantial endowments, the Dervishes have never, hke the monastic Orders of Christendom, departed from the original principles of their founders. Their manner of Hving is still as frugal as was that of the original Twelve Orders, and the architecture of their Tekkehs is marked by extreme simplicity both of form and material, any ornamental articles they may contain being the gifts of the pious; while their surplus revenues are either given directly to the poor in the shape of alms, or employed in the foundation of charitable institutions such as almshouses, schools, or baths.

When it happens that a Dervish has been raised to the rank of Sheikh by the General of his Order, without being appointed to the rule of a special Tekkeh, he is directed to take up his abode in some town which has been indicated to his Chief, by means of a dream or vision, as specially marked out for the establishment of a new community. Here he remains until the citizens, incited by a pious emulation, erect a Tekkeh and provide for its support. Most of the existing monasteries have sprung up in this way; and the practice, to some extent, still continues.

It is not unusual to find Mevlevi Sheikhs engaged in commercial pursuits, necessitated by the nature of the source from which their revenues are derived. For instance, if the vakouf consists of arable land, and is cultivated on the metayer system, the sale of the produce devolves on the Sheikh, who generally proves himself well able to fulfil the temporal, as well as the spiritual, duties of his office. I happened one day, after witnessing a performance of the Mevlevi Dervishes at Salonica, to make a remark to the Inspector of Customs on the prepossessing appearance and reverend bearing of the Sheikh, a handsome man in the prime of life. " Oh,

BEGGING DERVISH AND NIGHT-WATCHMAN he replied, laughing, Ne vous fiez pas a sa bonne physionomie; il ny a personne qui me donne plus dembarras dans les affaires." But even St. Theresa, it appears, was a very good business woman.

The great founder of this Order, to judge from the following anecdote, also knew how to turn his position to account for the advantage of his community:–

" Whenever the grandees of Konieh entertained a desire to have an audience of the Sheikh Shemsu 'd-Din of Tebriz, they would request Husam (Jelal's secretary) to procure it for them through the influence of his master with the Sheikh. Jelal and Hu am used to tax those nobles for this favour according to their means and circumstances. On one occasion the Grand Vizier solicited an audience, and was taxed at forty thousand pieces of silver; which sum, after much chaffering, was reduced to thirty thousand. At his audience with Shems, the Vizier was so charmed with the mysteries revealed to him that, on his return therefrom, he voluntarily sent to Hussm the ten thousand pieces of silver which had been abated from the sum originally fixed. These moneys were always expended by Husam as he saw fit, in relieving the necessities of the holy community, and the families of Jelal, the gold-beater (Husam), and their various dependents."

See Mrs. Cunningham Graham's Life of St. Theresa, 1894.

2 The Acts of the Adepts. Sir W. Redhouse's Translation. 6–(3119)

The Tekkehs of the Bektashis are unostentatious groups of buildings, consisting of cells for the brethren and a plain square hall for their common devotions. In the centre of the floor is a large dodecangular stone called the Maidan Tdsh, on which, during all their ceremonies except that of initiation, stands a lighted candle. Around this are twelve postakis, or sheepskin mats, significative of the twelve Imams; the one nearest to a niche in the wall which denotes the Kibleh, or direction of Mekka, being the seat of the Sheikh, and the others those of the eleven elders. The apartment reserved for the Sheikh is called the " cell of the master." He, however, unless under a vow of celibacy, seldom occupies it permanently, but resides with his family; and the rule of the convent in his absence devolves upon a deputy Sheikh, the senior of the celibates. Those of the Orders who for various reasons are, Hke the Hamzavis, under the ban of the ruhng powers, assemble in buildings undistinguishable externally from ordinary dwelling-houses.

The tombs of the Evliya, as Moslem saints are called, are held in religious veneration in all Mohammedan countries, and are honoured by the erection over them of Turbihs, or mausoleums. A Turbeh is usually a square edifice with a domed roof built over a sarcophagus of stone or brickwork, higher at the head than at the foot and rising in the centre to a ridge. To some Turbehs are attached apartments in which reside the Dervishes who have charge of them. The walls of these shrines have grated openings through which can be seen the tomb, often covered with rich shawls and carpets, the pious offerings of recipients of benefits beheved to have been bestowed through the mediation of the Saint buried there. On the gratings flutter innumerable httle coloured rags, portions of the clothing of rich persons who hope by this means to transfer their diseases to the Saint, or who leave them as votive tabellcb to remind him of the blessings hoped for through his mediation with Allah. In a niche in the masonry of the sarcophagus a small lamp, fed with sweet oil, is kept continually burning. These lamps symbohse the nur, or holy hght, which, it is said, is frequently seen to hover over the grave of a Saint, and has made known the resting-place of many holy Dervishes who have died while on journeys or pilgrimages.

Among the famous Sheikhs who held the post of guardian of a shrine was the Pir, Abdul Kadr Ghilani, the founder of the Kadiri Order. He had charge of the tomb of the celebrated Imam, Abu Khanife, at Bagdad, where he also was buried. And round the Turbeh of Abdul Kadr ("The Rose of Bagdad") are grouped in such numbers the domes that cover the mortal remains of the most renowned mystics of the East that the locahty is known to the present day as " The Grove of the Saints."

The Turbih at Broussa of the famous Dervish, Emir Sultan, is thus described by Evhya Eifendi, 1 See p. 18. 2 See p. 33.

who visited it towards the end of the seventeenth century.

" He is buried without Broussa to the east, beneath a lofty dome. The gates of the Turbeh are inlaid with silver, as also is the entrance, at which the visitor descends six steps. The walls are covered with variegated porcelain tiles. Four of the windows look westwards towards the plain of Broussa, and four towards the Kibleh (Mekka) into the yard of the Turbeh. The great number of suspended ornaments which adorn the interior of the mausoleum are equalled only in the Turbehs of Medina; the silken carpets are richer than are found anywhere else. The sarcophagus is surrounded by gold and silver lamps, candlesticks, and vases for holding perfumes and rosewater; on the richly-embroidered silken draperies which cover it lie Korans writ by the hands of famous scribes; and at the head a large turban stands majestically. Those who enter are struck with such awe that many do not dare to attempt it, but only look into it by a window at the head, and recite a Fatiha.

1 Narrative of Travels.

2 Though printing was introduced into Turkey more than a century and a half ago, a beautiful manuscript is at the present day preferred to a printed book, and many beautifully written and illuminated copies of the Koran are to be found in the country, as a prejudice still exists against printing the Sacred Book.

3 The first chapter of the Koran, the Moslem Paternoster. " Mohammedans look upon the Fatiha as the quintessence of the whole Koran, and often repeat it in their devotions both public and private." Sale, Al Koran, p. 1, note.

A village called Bektsshkeui, near Angora, contains the tomb of Hadji Bektash, the founder of the Bektashi Order. It stands in a commanding position overlooking the city, under the dome of a Turbeh, and close by is a Tekkeh occupied by a small community of Bektashi Dervishes. This shrine is naturally much venerated, and visited by pilgrims from all parts of the Empire. The front of the Tekkeh is embellished with a portico or verandah, supported on pillars of marble, and on the side of a well in the court visitors are shown indentations said to have been made by the teeth of the Saint, and in the doorway the impression of his hand. In the vicinity are salt mines which, tradition says, were miraculously created by Hadji Bektash, who, when passing through the village, had found the inhabitants suffering from a scarcity of that commodity. This village now bears the name of Touzkeui, the " Salt Village."

At Merdevenkeui, a village not far from the Asiatic suburb of Kadikeui, is the Turbeh of an eminent Bektashi saint, once a Chaoush, or messenger in the service of Sultan Achmet, which is much frequented by pious Moslems. Close by is a large stone said to possess the power of granting the wish of any person standing upon it. A Turkish lady of my acquaintance, the late Besmi Sultana, attributed her elevation to the high and exceptional position of legal wife of Sultan Abdul Medj id to the wish she mentally expressed when standing on this stone, after, of course, depositing her devotional offering on the neighbouring shrine of thc Evliyd,

Many Turbehs, however, consist merely of four roofless walls, pierced with grated openings, built round the sarcophagus. Some are to be found in the crowded thoroughfares of towns and cities, some by country roadsides, while others occupy corners of the pubhc burial grounds. At Salonica, one is situated at the entrance to the bazaar, and another curiously located in the cellar basement of a Jewish merchant's warehouse, the tomb being visible from the street through a grated opening close to the ground. The cost of the hghts always kept burning in these humbler shrines is defrayed either by some pious bequest, or by the offerings of the passers-by.

It is customary for a visitor, or pilgrim, on arriving at a turbeh, to greet its saintly occupant as he would a hving person with the beautiful Oriental salutation, "Peace be with you " (Salaam aleikum). He then recites a Fatiha before the entrance, and, walking round the grave from left to right, repeats it at each of the four sides. Sometimes a longer sura of the Koran is used, or, perhaps, as in the case of a devout Dervish on his pilgrimage, the whole of the Sacred Book. The recitation concludes with this collect, apparently addressed to the Saint: " Extol the perfection of thy Lord, the Lord of might, exempting Him from that which they 1 See above, p. 72.

Christians ascribe to Him " i. e. having a partaker of his Godhead.

These arts of devotion are generally performed for the sake of the Saint, though the merit of them is also beheved to reflect at the same time upon the pilgrim who makes the recitation, and adds the words " Peace be upon the Apostles and praise be to Allah, the Lord of all creatures. 0 Allah I I have transferred the merit of what I have recited from the excellent Koran to the soul of this Saint," When prayers are offered for some special blessing—which usually, if not for health or dehverance from some impending calamity, is of a purely worldly nature, such as the furtherance of some ambitious project, or the favour of the Sultan, or some other dignitary whose influence is required—the following, or some similar formula, is used: " 0 Allah! I conjure Thee by the Prophet, and by him to whom this place is dedicated, to grant me," etc. The hands of the suppliant are held upwards and open during the prayer, and, at its conclusion, passed over the face. Some fervent pilgrims, hke Evhya Effendi, kiss the threshold, others the walls, windows, and grave-coverings of the holy shrines.

The prayers of the guardians of Turbehs are also often soucited by those in need of spiritual consolation and assistance. These watchers of the holy dead are often Sheikhs who have abandoned the world for this purpose, and whose hves of undoubted purity exalt them to the position of intermediaries between the Saint and ordinary sinful men. They have often one or more disciples to assist them in their pious duties, who in due time succeed their spiritual guide in his office. The revenues are derived chiefly from the offerings of pilgrims, but in some cases iurbehsy like tekkehsy are endowed with landed property.

The tombs of Christian saints, strange to say, come in for their share of the general hagiolatry, though, as the Christians also patronise Moslem saints, this is but a quid pro quo. The beautiful basilica of St. Dimitri at Salonica, built in the fifth century over the miracle-working tomb of that Saint, was, in 1180, for the second time, converted into a mosque. On the removal of the Ayia Tpdire a—the Holy Table of the Greek Church—the relics which had had their resting-place beneath it were reverently removed to a cell at the north-west corner of the narthex. The Greeks and other Christians are now allowed to visit this shrine freely; and the old Mevlevi Dervish, who acts as caretaker of the mosque, appears to have no less faith in the miraculous powers of St. Dimitri than have the numerous members of the Orthodox Church who make pilgrimages to his shrine. One of my visits to this ancient Metropolitan Church was paid in company with a Greek matron who, having been educated in Germany and France, was a thorough sceptic in such matters. Seeing that we were strangers, the Dervish enumerated in his broken Greek the virtues and antiquity of the Saint. He then fumbled under the tombstone and produced a handful of earth and what looked like a long mesh of cotton candlewick. Having ascertained from my friend her name, and the names of her husband, father-in-law, and children, the old man slowly repeated them, tying at each name a knot in the cotton over the flame of the candle burning on the tomb, and then presented her with this girdle with the assurance that, if worn on the person it would relieve her or them of any of the ills to which the flesh is heir. I was also the fortunate recipient of a small quantity of greasy earth, from which I was promised similar benefits.

1 An odoriferous unguent (fivpov) is said to exude from the bones of certain saints who from this circumstance are called ij. vpob vtai. St. Nicholas is one of these myroblites. Sir John Maunderville, speaking of the relics of St. Catharine, on Mount Sinai, says, "The prelate of the Monkes schewethe the Relykes to the Pilgrymes. And with an Instrument of Sylver, he frotethe the Bones: and thanne ther gothe out a lytylle Oyle, as thoughe it were in a maner swetynge, that is nouther like to Oyle ne to Bawme; but it is fulle swete of smelle." (Quoted by Mr. Athelstan Riley in Mount Athos, p. 127 n.)

CHAPTER V

MONASTIC RULE AND DISCIPLINE

" Who Poverty's low door to enter eer has sought, Aye to his death beneath its roof remains,

Lays greed aside, and, as a monarch reigns;

For proud the station is of him who needeth naught."

A Dervish Tekkeh, or convent, usually contains from fifteen to thirty disciples, ruled over by a Sheikh. The Sheikh has unlimited power and authority in the Tekkeh. If it is endowed with vakouf property, he sells the produce of the farms, regulates the expenditure of the Tekkeh, and distributes its alms. If his convent is unendowed, he looks for its support to the pious and charitable– the " Friends of Allah." For, occupied as he is supposed continually to be with spiritual matters, a Sheikh cannot, like his disciples, follow a worldly avocation, but must live–according to the Dervish expression–" on the Doorstep of Allah." The disciples are also expected to contribute to his support and to the other expenses of the Tekkeh: and it is usual for them to bring some small present every time they visit him. As every detail of convent life is symbolical, this custom is said to commemorate the offerings brought by Gabriel to Adam, after his expulsion from Paradise, and which, the legend says, consisted of a kind of small loaves and corn,

MONASTIC RULE AND DISCIPLINE 79 with parrots and turtle doves for his entertainment, and swallows and hens for that of Eve.

Each Order has its Chief Sheikh, or General, who resides in the city or town which contains the tomb of its founder (Pir), and is considered the guardian of the sacred relics. Bagdad, as mentioned in the preceding chapter, is the burial place of Abdul Kadr Ghilani, the founder of the Kadiri Order, and his eminence in the Dervish world caused many succeeding Pirs to choose their place of sepulture in the neighbourhood of his tomb. This city is, consequently, a great centre of Dervish Generals. Konieh (Iconium), in Asia Minor, is the seat of the Mevlevi General, the successor and lineal descendant of the talented Jelalu-'d-Din. For the dignity of Sheikh is hereditary in the Mevlevi, Bektashi, and Kadiri Orders. If the son be a minor at the death of his father, one of the elders is elected to act as his deputy (Naih Khalifeh) until he reaches the age of twenty. In the other Orders a council of Sheikhs, presided over by the General, choose a new Prior from among the disciples of the deceased Murshid, who do not appear to have any voice in the matter. Their choice falls, as a rule, on the elder who has so distinguished himself by his 1 The Mohammedan legend says that the swallows were the means of reconciliation between Adam and Eve after their expulsion from Paradise when they had gone different ways. They found out Adam in Ceylon, and brought a hair of his beard to Eve who was at Jedda, returning with one of her hairs to Adam; and the pair met on Mount Arafat, near Mekka.

spiritual advancement as to have previously held the post of Deputy Sheikh; or, if such a functionary is not to be found in the convent, on one of the elders, generally the senior. The nomination is then notified to the Sheikh-ul-Islam, or Grand Mufti, from whose hands a new Prior must receive his investiture, even when he succeeds to the rule of a convent by right of heredity. This is, however, merely a matter of form, being a nominal acknowledgment of the Sheikh-ul-Islam as the spiritual head (under the Sultan) of the Mohammedan world; for custom and prejudice have rendered it almost impossible for that dignitary to refuse to invest a Sheikh chosen by the Dervish primates. According to the rules of a few Orders, a Prior is free to leave his mantle of succession at his death to the disciple whom he may deem most worthy of it; and in those Orders in which the office is hereditary in the family of its founder, if the Sheikh leave no son or immediate heir, the heads of several convents of the same Order meet and choose a successor; or the members of his community elect one of their own number, generally the senior, to the vacant office. Such a choice is not, however, made without much dehberation, fasting, and prayer for divine guidance; and, consequently, there is no unseemly rivalry among the brethren, for the result of their prayers and deliberations is looked upon as the revelation of the will of Allah, and their choice, made with such solemnity, is consequently ratified by the Grand Mufti without demur.

AN ELDER OF THE MEVLEVI ORDER
MONASTIC RULE AND DISCIPLINE 81
Many of the Dervish Sheikhs are Seyyids, or Hneal descendants of the family of the Prophet, through the grandsons of his nephew and son-in-law, the Khahf AU, who escaped the massacre in which their fathers, Hasan and Husam–" The Martyrs "– lost their Hves. Seyyids are distinguished by their green turbans, and enjoy pecuhar privileges. They are not under the same jurisdiction as ordinary Mussulmans, but are ruled by a functionary called the Nakeb-el-Eshref, who resides at Constantinople. Everyone claiming to be a descendant of the Prophet is required to possess a document estabhshing his genealogy.

If a Sheikh is a cehbate, he resides in the convent, where a special apartment called the " cell of the Master " is reserved for his use. Many of the heads of convents, however, are married, though it is considered necessary for them to receive, in a vision, a spiritual dispensation before taking to themselves wives; and such Priors appoint deputies to rule over the monastic brethren in the convents during their absence. Like most Ottomans of the present day they are, as a rule, monogamists, but not always, nor are their wives always saintly women. Some years ago I paid a visit to the harem of the Mevlevi Prior of Magnesia (ad Sipylum), in Asia Minor, who ranks next in the

Order to the General at Konieh. He had two wives. The Bash Kadin, or first wife, to whom he had been married some years, but who was childless, was dark-haired and handsome, but with a rather haughty and ill-tempered expression, increased, perhaps, by the thick eyebrows painted to meet over the nose. The second wife, not long a bride, was of the fair Circassian type, brown-haired and blue-eyed, and evidently a little in awe of her imperious-looking companion. We were also courteously received in the selamlik by the Sheikh, a handsome man in the prime of life whose dignified presence was enhanced by his flowing mantle of hght fawn-coloured cloth and his tall Dervish hat. One of his neophytes, a fine youth of seventeen or thereabouts, was, as we took our leave, commissioned by his Murshid to show us some of the sights of the town. Magnesia being built on the lower slopes of Mount Sipylus, its upper streets are so steep that they are terraced into staircases. As we toiled upwards, the young Dervish, who was kindly carrying a little girl belonging to our party, was asked by a group of children whom we passed, "Are you not ashamed to be going about with Giaours? " The neophyte made no reply, but turned again with an apologetic smile to continue his conversation with the mother of the little girl. Had this mere boy already learned the main precept of his Order, which may be summed up in the one word– Love?

The domestic peace of another married Sheikh at Adrianople was much disturbed by the unruly temper of his wife. The garden of his house adjoined that of an English lady, who, though she maintained friendly relations with the holy man, was MONASTIC RULE AND DISCIPLINE 83 very often disturbed by the cries of his passionate and ill-tempered spouse. Nor could the good man make use of his privilege of divorce to rid himself of his uncongenial helpmeet, as he was not in a position to pay the sum promised in the marriage contract (nekyah) in case of such a contingency.

Early one morning my friend was disturbed by cries of " Fire " (Yangen var f) proceeding from- the Sheikh's abode. Snatching up a can of water, she hastened downstairs, and, followed by her servants with pails, entered her neighbour's premises through a gate in the garden wall. No indications of a conflagration were, however, visible. But in front of the house stood the Dervish with his ebony armrest in his hand, while on the ground sat his wife, sobbing hysterically; and it was only too evident that the holy man's patience had been at last tried beyond further endurance, and that he had administered the correction that had been only too long deserved.

To arrive at the degree of spirituality required in those who fill the office of Deputy Prior, a Dervish must have spent much time in prayer, fasting, and complete abstraction from all worldly pursuits. Besides being far advanced on the spiritual path, and familiar with all the mystical dogmas and tenets of the Order, he must possess the respect, reverence, and entire submission of the rest of the community. By constant prayer and the continued performance of the Zikr, his breath, and even his touch, should have acquired a sanctifying and heahng influence, and he must also be believed to possess the power of working miracles. He will be favoured with visions, and by their import his superior is able to judge when his spiritual training may be considered complete, when he terminates the period of his seclusion. He will then commence his pilgrimage to the holy cities and the tombs of the saints, and, perhaps, may proceed as far as Bagdad, if the founder of his Order be among the many saints buried there, when it will also be his duty to visit the burial place of the grandsons of the Prophet at Kerbeleh, in the vicinity of that city.

Each of the twelve members of a Bektashi fraternity has some special office attached to his postaki (sheepskin seat). Some of these would appear to entail a certain amount of manual labour, while others have merely nominal, or at most only occasional, duties. They are as follows:— 1. The Sheikh. 8. The Bagbearer.

2. The Cook. 9. The Sacrificer.

3. The Baker. 10. The attendant of the 4. The Deputy Shekh. Tekkeh.

5. The Superintendent. 11. The Groom.

6. The Steward. 12, The attendant on the 7. The Coffee-maker. guests.

1 Commemorative of Kamber, the groom of the Khalif Ali.

MONASTIC RULE AND DISCIPLINE 85

The other Orders appear to have officers more or less similar to these attached to the service of the convent.

Though all Dervishes are free to leave the Order into which they have originally entered and join another, or even to return to the world, it is very rare that any use is made of the hberty. Each member seems to regard it as a sacred duty to remain faithful for life to the Order that first received him, and in its dress to end his days. To this spirit of devotion they add that of perfect submission to the will of their Prior. " Consider your guide (Murshid) as the greatest of all guides," and " Whatever you do or think, let your Sheikh be always present to your mind," are two primary obhgations expressed by a formula called the rabouta, which is repeated by them as scrupulously as is the namdz by the orthodox Mohammedans. Humihty of spirit and demeanour are required from all; they are taught not to consider themselves superior to others, but to rank themselves as the poorest, lowest, and most humble of mankind. Hence, not only in the cloister, but in all their deahngs with the outer world, these mystics are distinguished by the deep humihty of their manner. Their heads are ever bent, their gaze absorbed; and the words Ay V Allah (Thanks to God) are ever upon their lips. They must not divulge the secrets of the Order to their wives or relatives, nor to anyone who is not, like them, a " seeker after the Truth."

Special forms of salutation are used by the 7–(2119)

Dervishes. As the Love of God is the principal of the Mevlevis, their salutation is " Let it be Love! " (Eshk olsoun); but that in general use among the Orders is " Ya Hoo " (O Him). After the reception of a Dervish into an Order the only salutation required of him on entering the Tekkeh is to incline his head gently towards the Sheikh, and lay the right hand across the breast near the neck, in token of perfect submission to him. It is said that brethren not in costume recognise each other in public by placing the right hand, as if accidentally, on the chin. It is also customary for Dervishes when entering the Tekkeh or on meeting each other, to place the right hand on the heart, and, gently inchning the body, to exclaim " Yd Hoo, Evens I " (O Him, Brethren), the reply to which is'Ay Vallah, Shahim (Good, by Allah, my Shah). On making an enquiry concerning the health, they say, "Health, my Joys! " and the reply is " Good, by Allah, my brother." Their other salutations on meeting and taking leave are Hoo, dost Erenler (Him, dear friend), and Aye Vallah Hoo dost. Towards those who are not

Dervishes they, however, use the ordinary beautiful Mohammedan greeting. Salaam aleikoum (Peace be to thee).

There are special prayers and formulas for every event and detail of convent life. Those of the Bektashis are seventy-six in number, and are called by the symbolical name of " Interpreters." On crossing the doorsill of the Tekkeh, they say:–

" I have placed my head and my heart on the

MONASTIC RULE AND DISCIPLINE 87 sill of the door of repentance, so that my body may be pure as gold. Deign, O Sheikh, to turn your eyes for an instant on this poor man (faqir).

On presenting an offering to his superior, the disciple says:–

" The ant brought as an offering to Solomon the thigh of a grasshopper. Thou, O Sheikh, art Solomon, and I am thy ant; accept my humble offering."

On asking for hospitahty at a Tekkeh, or Turbeh, the traveller says:–

" Allah is our Friend! Peace to the dwellers in this Tekkeh. Love to those who are joyful, and to all the poor men (fouqara) now present; to the Pirs and to the Sheikhs; to the dwellers in this house of the Shah (AH)."

The grace before meals of the Bektashis differs from that used by the Kadiris and the generality of the Orders. It runs thus:–

" O Allah! 0 Allah! By the horn of the archangel Israfeel! by the symbolism of Kamber! by the hght of the Prophet! by the altar and the pulpit! by our sovereign Pir, Hadji Bektash Vali! by our General! by the breath nefs) of the Three, the Five, the Seven, and the Forty True Saints, we thank Thee. Hoo!"

The following is the grace used by the Kadiris. That of the other Orders differs from it only in the name of the founder:–

" Praise be to Allah! May He increase His bounties. By the blessings of Abraham! By the

Light of the Prophet! By the grace of Ah! By the war cry of Mohammed! By the secret of Abdul Kadr Ghilani, we beseech Thee to be gracious to our Lord (the Pr)."

It is a rule of the Order of the Hamzavis, obligatory on all members, to retain in their minds during their meals, both when with others as well as when alone, a continual remembrance of God; and after they have eaten, to offer devout thanks.

Notwithstanding that all the Orders are nominally mendicant, and dependent for subsistence on the offerings of the pious, begging is strictly forbidden, save among the Bektashis and wandering Dervishes. These, who deem it meritorious to live upon alms, frequent the bazaars and pubuc streets for the purpose of recommending themselves to the charity of passers-by. Their formula of request is generally " Something, for the love of Allah." Many Bektashis, however, make it a rule to support themselves by handicraft trades, and particularly by making, in imitation of their Pir, Hadji Bektash, small articles of wood, such as spoons, ladles, bowls, and graters. They also carve out of pieces of marble the fastenings used by Dervishes of that order for their belts and for the collars of their garments, and fashion the two-beaked bowls (keshgool) used by the mendicants when soliciting alms. The monastic brethren belonging to the other and endowed Orders are supphed only with food and lodging at the expense of the Tekkeh. Their meals, which are very simple, and consist, as a rule, of two dishes only, are usually

MONASTIC RULE AND DISCIPLINE 89 eaten in the solitude of the cells; but on certain occasions the brethren dine together in the common room. Each Dervish is required to provide himself with dress and other necessaries, and, though hving in the convent, follows some trade or profession. Those who are good calligraphists find employment in copying the Koran and other rehgious books. If any are without resources, they seldom fail to receive contributions either from their relations, an allowance from the Prior, or a pension from some wealthy individual. For although, as above remarked, the members of the majority of the Order are forbidden to ask for alms, they are allowed to accept gifts when offered by charitable persons " for the love of Allah." The rule against begging appears also to be relaxed in the case of Dervishes on their pilgrimage, as they are then usually without their ordinary means of support. Many Mohammedans reserve their alms exclusively for the Dervishes, and make it their duty to seek out those of high reputation for sanctity, visit them frequently, and supply their wants. Others, again, even lodge and board holy men in their houses, in the hope of thus drawing upon themselves, their families, and their fortunes the blessings of heaven.

All married Dervishes reside with their famihes, but sleep in the convent once or twice a week on the nights preceding their religious exercises. No married Dervish is, however, allowed to pass the night in the Tekkeh of the Mevlevi General at Konieh. The lay brethren, after passing their novitiate in the Tekkeh, return to their ordinary avocations; withdrawing, however, as much as possible from all intercourse with the world, and endeavouring to lead spiritual and holy hves.

Various forms of punishment and penance are imposed on erring Dervishes by their Sheikh according to the gravity of the offence. Evhya Effendi says that when a disciple has committed any fault or breach of discipline, he is judged by a council composed of the Prior and the elders, and sentenced to a term of imprisonment not exceeding three days, as a longer period of incarceration might be detrimental to his family and worldly affairs. The council are, however, careful to examine well into any accusation, and not to punish the defaulter too severely. In former times the bastinado was inflicted by the Sheikh on his erring disciples. He was, however, required, when striking, never to lift the stick higher than his ear, to do which was reckoned " mere injustice and passionate behaviour." Another punishment was that of carrying a heavy stone suspended round the neck, a custom which is said to have originated with Moses. It is a sin for a Dervish to speak a word which is contrary to the four " gates," or principles of Justice, Truth, Order, and Knowledge. One who speaks useless or purposeless words is said to have strayed from the Path (Tariq). This general habit of reticence is variously illustrated in Dervish writings. " A Dervish, when asked by one of his brethren what 1 See p, 115.

MONASTIC RULE AND DISCIPLINE 91 marvellous gift he had brought back with him from the garden of delights he had visited in his ecstatic trance, rephed: I intended, on arriving at the Rosebush (the presence of Allah) to fill the skirt of my robe with roses, in order to offer them to my brethren on my return. But when I arrived at the Rosebush, its odour so intoxicated my senses that the hem of my robe escaped from my grasp. Silent is the tongue of the man who has known Allah.

It is also related of Jelalu-'d-Dm that when one day on a visit to a fellow Sheikh of great repute, he was asked by a Dervish who happened to be present, "What is Poverty? Jelal returned no answer, and the question was thrice repeated. When the poet left, the Sheikh, after accompanying him to the door, returned to the Dervish and severely reprimanded him for his insolent intrusion on his distinguished guest, which, he said, " was the more inexcusable as he (Jelal) fully answered thy question the first time thou didst put it." The Dervish, surprised, asked what the answer had been. " A poor man (faqir)' rephed the Prior, " is one who, having known Allah, hath his tongue tied."

Many Dervishes voluntarily practise a most rigid abstinence. Those of the Khalveti Order occasionally perform a painful fast of forty days' duration, living during that period on bread and water alone. As mentioned in a preceding chapter, the word Khalvet signifies " retirement," and the Sheikh of that name who founded this Order practised it to a great extent. Devout Dervishes in all the Orders condemn themselves to the performance of acts of the utmost austerity, and remain for a long time shut up in their cells for the purposes of prayer and meditation. Certain nights being considered pecuharly holy as anniversaries of some event in the life of the Prophet, these are specially consecrated to penitence and prayer. In order to drive away sleep, some will stand for whole nights in constrained attitudes; others, in order to maintain themselves in a sitting posture, tie their hair to a cord hanging from the ceiling, a practice called chilleh; others again fasten their limbs together with a leather strap passed round their necks and holding the knees up to the chin.

If a Dervish, when on his pilgrimage to the holy places, neglects or fails to perform any of the prescribed rites and ceremonies attached to that sacred duty, he atones for it by a sacrifice. On the same principle, a Dervish who finds himself guilty under other circumstances of a sin of omission or commission, brands himself with a hot iron in order to avoid the punishment of purgatorial fires in the next world. According to Evhya Effendi, " those 1 See above, p. 18.

2 For instance, the anniversary of the Prophet's birth; the 27th night of Ramazan, called the " Night of Power," at one moment of which, according to popular belief, all inanimate things–trees, plants and mountains–bow themselves in adoration of Allah, and all waters taste sweet; and the " Excellent Night," the 10th of the month of Shaban when the Recording Angels deliver up their books to the Almighty, and commence new ones.

MONASTIC RULE AND DISCIPLINE 93 who have a hundred and one scars on their heads proclaim that they have tried a hundred and one spiritual paths, and have abandoned everything connected with the world; those who wear on their foreheads the scar of resignation signify by it that they cherish in their hearts no desire but Allah; those who brand their ears, that they have renounced their own wills and Hve only to fulfil that of Allah."

Every convent, and every shrine at which a Dervish resides, has one or more guest-chambers which are at the disposal of traveuing Dervishes of any Order, and in which, especially if no other place of refuge is at hand, other Mussulmans on their pilgrimage arc madc welcome. It is the special duty of one of the brethren to attend upon the guests, bring them food from the common kitchen, and perform the other Httle rites of Oriental hospitahty, such as making their coffee and preparing their chibouks for smoking. If the guest be a Sheikh, he is received in the apartment of the Superior of the convent, and otherwise treated with special consideration.

The funeral of a Dervish Sheikh of high repute is a most impressive and interesting ceremony. Besides his own congregation, the members of other Orders in the neighbourhood, together with a large concourse of the male population, assemble at the Tekkeh to follow the departed to his last resting-place. After the usual burial service, called the mihit namdz, has been performed in the monastery, four or more of the disciples of the deceased Sheikh take up on their shoulders the rude coffin, which is covered with shawls, and bears at the head his turban. The bereaved fraternity proceed slowly towards the cemetery, uttering at intervals the exclamation, "AUah! Allah!" Behind follows the long and irregular procession, winding along the narrow streets. In the Turkish quarter the women peep through their latticed bhnds with reverent curiosity, and in the Christian mahallahs lean out of their open windows to watch its progress. There are Mevlevi Dervishes in tall hats and flowing mantles; Bektashis in close round caps and black robes; orthodox Imams in their ample white turbans; and townspeople of every creed in multicoloured garments, with here and there a soldier or official in tasselled fez, all pacing with bowed heads and sedate looks. If a mosque or Tekkeh is passed on the route, the coffin is deposited in front of the gateway and a service chanted, the whole assembly solemnly joining in the refrain of Amin! Amin! A fresh relay of bearers then raises the coffin, and the solemn procession moves on.

CHAPTER VI

THE STAGES OF INITIATION

" And he who hopes to scale the heights Without enduring pain, And toil, and strife, but wastes his life In idle quest and vain."

The founder of one of the earliest Orders of Dervishes, Sheikh Olwan, laid down certain rules to be observed in the admission of new members into his Brotherhood; and these rules, though subsequently elaborated by certain of the Orders, are still substantially the same in their leading features, differing only in the severity of the disciphne imposed upon a candidate, in the length of his period of probation, and in certain minor details.

As a general rule, a neophyte is required during his novitiate to hve in complete retirement from the world, to perform the menial offices of the Tekkeh, and to repeat daily 101, 151, or 301 times one of the attributes of the Deity. These are ninety-seven in number, and are called the Isdmi Ilahi, or " Beautiful Names of Allah." Seven only of these are used by a Murid; they are La ilaha il Allah (" There is no God but Allah "); Ya Allah (" O God "); Ya Hoo (" O Him "); Yd Hakk (" O Truth "); Yd Hay (" O Ever Living "); Yd Kayyoum (" O Self-existent "); and Yd Kahhar (" O Almighty"). In the first stage of his probation the neophyte repeats only the first attribute, and his advancement through the seven successive stages depends upon the proofs he is able to give of the reahty of his vocation for a Dervish hfe. These proofs are found in the frequency and vividness of the dreams and visions vouchsafed to him, which he is bound to communicate to his Superior.

Admission into the Mevlevi Order is only obtained by the performance of an uninterrupted novitiate of a thousand and one consecutive days. Should the Murid fail in a single day's duties, or be absent from the Tekkeh for one whole night, his probation must be re-commenced; and, whatever his worldly rank, he must consider himself the subordinate of every member of the Tekkeh. He is instructed in his duties by the Ashjihashi, or Chief of the Kitchen, spends much of his time in prayer and fasting, and in committing to memory the prayers and passages of the Koran more especially used by his Order. He must also become proficient in the mystic dance, and take part in the pubhc services of the Brotherhood. The novice, having passed through his period of probation to the satisfaction of the Chief of the Kitchen, that functionary–who acts as his sponsor–reports him to the Sheikh as worthy of admission to the initiatory grade of the Order, and a meeting of all the Brotherhood is convened in the Ismi Jelih Hufreh, the private assembly room of the Tekkeh. When all are assembled, the Murid is led by the Ashjihashi to the Prior, who occupies the seat of honour in the angle of the divan; he kisses the extended hand of his Superior, and seats himself on the floor before him. His sponsor then places his right hand on the neck, and his left on the forehead of the neophyte, the Sheikh takes off the kulah which, with the rest of the Mevlevi costume he has worn during his novitiate, and proceeds to chant a Persian distich composed by the founder of the Order. He then delivers an exhortation to the young disciple, at the termination of which he replaces the kulah on his head. The Murid and his sponsor now place themselves in the middle of the room, where they assume a posture of profound humihty, standing with folded arms, crossed toes, and bowed heads. The Ashjihashi is then addressed as follows by the Sheikh:–

" May the services of the Murid, thy brother, be agreeable to the Throne of the Eternal, and in the eyes of our Pir; may His satisfaction, His felicity, and His glory grow in the nest of the humble, in the cell of the poor. Let us exclaim Hoo (Him) in honour of our Mevlana. The Murid and his sponsor answer " Hoo! " and the former then kisses the hand of the Sheikh, who addresses to him some paternal remarks on his new position, and concludes by asking all the members of the congregation to embrace and welcome their new brother.

A novice of the Bektashi Order is also required to perform a novitiate of a thousand and one days, during which he frequents the services of the Tekkeh. But the formalities observed by this Order in the reception of candidates differ from those of 1 The founder of the Order, Mevlana Jelalu-'d-Din.

the Mevlevi Brethren, and are even more elaborate. A candidate is recommended to the Sheikh by two members of the community who are called his " Interpreters." 1 He must also have already given during his novitiate proofs of spiritual knowledge and acquirements, and have faithfully kept certain pretended secrets of the Order imparted to him as tests of his powers of reticence. His reception into the Brotherhood is also determined by the revelations concerning him received, in dreams or visions, by the Sheikh from the Pir or from Ali. What is thus revealed is not communicated to the neophyte.

On the evening appointed for the ceremony of initiation–for the services of the Bektashi Order are always held by night–the neophyte takes with him to the convent a sheep and a small sum of money. The sheep is sacrificed on the threshold of the Tekkeh, pait of its wool is twisted into a rope, the rest being preserved to be made later on into a girdle for his use. If the candidate desires to take the vow of cehbacy, he is stripped naked; but if he proposes, as in the generahty of cases, to take only the ordinary, or secular vow of this widespread and numerous Order, his breast only is bared. With the rope round his neck he is led by his " Interpreters," one of whom carries the symbol termed the tebber, a kind of battle-axe, into the hall of the Tekkeh. Here he stands with his arms folded 1 Terjumdn. This term also signifies the secret password or phrase of the Bektashi Order.

MEVLEVI NEOPHYTE LEARNING THE DEVR across his breast, his hands on his shoulders, his toes crossed, and his body inchned towards the Sheikh– a posture signifying abject humihty and designated buyun kesmek. The Prior and the Twelve Elders are seated around the hall on their sheepskins, a lighted candle being placed in front of each. One of the Interpreters" announces to the Prior that he has brought to him a slave, and requests his acceptance of the gift. He acquiesces, and the neophyte, addressing him, repeats this prayer:–

" I have erred; pardon my fault, O Shah! For the sake of the Accepted One (Ah) of the Exalted Place; for the sake of the Martyr (Hussein). I have done wrong to myself, and to our Lord, and I implore pardon of Him."

His " fault " is supposed to consist in having so long delayed to join the Order. The Sheikh then recites a sort of Litany, to which the Murid makes the responses.

" In the Name of Allah, the Merciful and the Clement:–

" I beseech Allah's forgiveness (thrice repeated); I have come to implore pardon; I have come in search of the Truth; I ask it for the sake- of the Just. Truth is the path which leads to Allah, the All True, whom I know. What you term Evil, I also know to be Evil, and I will avoid taking with my hands what is another's. Repent of your sins unto Allah, a repentance that knows not return unto sin."

Then follows an exhortation by the Superior:–

" Eat nothing forbidden; speak no falsehood; quarrel with none; be kind to your inferiors; overlook the faults of others, and conceal them. If you cannot do this with your hand, do it with your skirts, your tongue, and your heart."

The novice then kisses the hand of the Sheikh, who continues:–

" If thou now accept me as thy father, I accept thee as my son. Be hereafter the pledge of Allah breathed in thy right ear."

He then repeats after his Superior the words: " Mohammed is my leader, and Ah is my guide." The Sheikh asks, "Dost thou accept me as thy Guide (meaning as the representative of Ah)? " to which he responds, "I accept thee as my Guide "; and the Sheikh adds, Then I accept thee as my son."

The postulant is now led by his " Interpreters to the Sheikh, before whom he first bows low and then prostrates himself, touching the floor with his forehead. Kneehng opposite to him so closely that their knees touch, the Superior takes the postulant's right hand in his, and the thumbs are raised to represent the Arabic letter Alif. The latter places his ear to the mouth of the Sheikh who imparts to him in a whisper the Ikrdndmeh, or secret Vows of the Order. As the tenets of the Bektashis are beheved by many to be purely pantheistic, it is asserted that the words whispered by the Sheikh to the Murid convey a doctrine to which he must

THE STAGES OF INITIATION 101 assent on pain of death, and admit the unity of God and Nature. But this assertion is positively denied by others; and it would, indeed, be difficult to prove it, as the secrets of the Order are never committed to writing, and are known only to its members, who, it is believed, are deterred by the most frightful penalties from divulging them.

When the disciple is presented with the girdle and the stone worn in it, the Prior, as he binds it round his waist says to him: "I now bind up thy waist in the path of Allah–O Holy Name, possessed of all knowledge! Whoever knows this Name will become the successor of his Sheikh (Naib). Certain principles of the Order are then imparted to the novice, who is also instructed in various mystic tenets concerning the universe and the Koran. The Sheikh then sums up by saying, "There is but one Light, and the Truth is (as) the Moon. He who has found the science of his own body (called the Hum i Vurgood, his spiritual counterpart) knows his Lord; for the holy Prophet has said, To know thyself is to know thy Lord. In this is comprised a knowledge of thine own secret, and that of thy Creator."

When a Bektashi takes the vow of celibacy, he is asked by the Sheikh whether, if he break it, he is willing to come under the sword of Ali, to which he replies in the affirmative. The inner signification of this phrase is said to contain one of the secret 1 See above, p. 36.

8–(2119) vows of the Order. On putting on for the first time the sash or Alif-lam, he says, "I abandon all matrimony, and bind myself by this sash so to do." The Murid then recites chapter cxii of the Koran; after which the Sheikh declares to him that " Allah doth not engender or bring forth, and so may men tell of thee, and no one is equal to Him."

Twelve being the Bektashi mystical number, a member having broken a vow, incurs twelve punishments. One of their secret signs is said to consist of the words Tehran and Toolan–" far " and " near "–signifjing " near in affection and far in conceit."

The ceremonies of affihation of the other Orders bear a great resemblance to the foregoing, with the exception of those of the Kddiri, the Rufah, the Sd di.

A novice of the Rufah receives from the Sheikh a small cup of water from the Zemzem–the Sacred Well of Mekka–which, after reciting a prayer over, he drinks.

At the initiation of a Sddi Dervish, a number of dates are placed before the Superior. He selects one, extracts the stone, breathes upon the fruit and puts it into the mouth of the neophyte who is seated on the floor before him. Two members of the Order seat themselves to the right and left of him, and proceed to sway him from side to side, reciting at the same time: "There is no God but Allah," the Sheikh doing the same, until he has swallowed the date. All then rise, and the Murid, after kissing 1 The first and last letters of the Arabic alphabet.

THE STAGES OF INITIATION 103 the hand of the superior, is acknowledged as a brother by the rest of the congregation.

A person wishing to join the Kddiri Order intimates his desire to one of its members. The Dervish enjoins him to frequent the Tekkeh and its services, and also to wait upon the brethren and their guests. These menial duties are required from every neophyte, whatever his worldly rank may be. The period of probation lasts for many months, during which time the Murid becomes greatly attached to his Superior. When he has been deemed worthy to enter the ranks of the Dervishes, he is directed to procure a cap of plain white felt, which is carried by his sponsor to the Sheikh. A gul, or piece of cloth stamped into the shape of a rose of eighteen petals, and having in the centre the " Solomon's Seal "–two interlaced triangles–is then attached to it. When the brethren assemble in the Tekkeh for the performance of the Zikr, or invocation of Allah, the Sheikh takes his place on his sheepskin and the neophyte, led by his sponsor, kneels before him and kisses his hand. The Sheikh takes off the novice's ordinary cap, and replaces it by that bearing the " Rose," which he has carried in his bosom, and says, three times, "Allahu Ekber " (God is Great).

A disciple does not, however, even after this formal reception into it, become at once a full member of the Order. This grade is only reached after, it may be, years of further probation, and its attainment depends upon the proofs he is able to give of his progress in spirituality. His final admission to full brotherhood is usually determined by a revelation from the Pir, or from Ah, received simultaneously by himself and his Sheikh. While passing through these intermediate stages, the aspirant is under the guidance of the Superior or of an initiate who has himself reached the highest degree. During the first stage, which is termed Sheridt, or " the Law," the disciple observes all the usual rites of Moslem worship, obeys all the commands and precepts of the Koran like any other True Behever, and is treated by the Brethren of the community as an uninitiated outsider. He is taught at the same time to concentrate his thoughts so completely on his " Guide " as to become mentally absorbed in him as a spiritual link with the supreme object of all devotion. This Guide must be the neophyte's shield against all worldly thoughts and desires; his spirit must aid him in all his efforts, accompany him wherever he may be, and be ever present to his mental vision. Such a frame of mind is termed " annihilation into the Murshid, and the Guide discovers, by means of his own visions, the degree of spirituality to which his disciple has attained, and to what extent his soul has become absorbed into his own.

The Murid now enters upon what, in Dervish phraseology, is called " the Path." During this period, which forms in reality the transition from outward to hidden things, the disciple is familiarised with those philosophical writings of the great

THE STAGES OF INITIATION 105

Sufi masters which form the chief subject of the lectures and studies of the Order. He is taught to substitute spiritual for ritual worship, and led by degrees to abandon the dogmas and formulas of Islam as necessary only for the unenlightened masses. This method is, however, pursued with great tact and caution, for a disciple is not released from the usual observances of religion until he has given proof of sincere piety, virtue, exceptional spirituality, and extreme asceticism; and a Dervish at this stage of his novitiate passes most of his time in solitary contemplation, endeavouring to detach his mind from all visible objects in order to attain the desired union with the Deity. His Guide, meanwhile, imparts to him his own mystical philosophy as he finds him capable of receiving it. If the disciple's religious feelings appear to be shocked by any maxim to which he has given utterance, the already mentioned Jesuitical expedient known as the Ketman supplies the Master with a double sense which enables him at once to convince his disciple of the groundlessness of his objections. If, on the contrary, the Murshid finds his pupil's theological digestion robust, his advance on the path will be correspondingly rapid. He is now supposed to come under the spiritual influence of the Pir, or founder of the Order, in whom he in turn becomes mentally absorbed to such a degree as to be virtually one with him, acquiring his attributes and power of performing supernatural acts.

The next stage of the mystic life is that termed by the Dervishes " Spiritual Knowledge," and the disciple who believes himself, and is beheved by his Sheikh to have attained to such knowledge or, in other words, to have become inspired, is held to be on an equahty with the Angels. He now enters into spiritual communion with the Prophet himself, into whose soul his own has become absorbed.

The fourth degree is usually attained during the forty days of fasting and seclusion, observed by every Dervish during his novitiate. In his ecstatic state he beheves himself to have become a part of the Divinity, and sees Him in all things. The Sheikh, after witnessing this remarkable proof of the success of his teachings, gently awakens the disciple from his ecstasy, and having restored him to his normal condition, bestows upon him the rank of khalifeh (" successor "). The mystic now resumes his outward observance of the rites of Islam, and prepares for his pilgrimage to the Holy Cities.

Not every Dervish, however, attains even to the third grade; and the highest is attained only by the few. Those less spiritually gifted, or less mystically minded, still continue to recognise the personal and anthropomorphic Allah of the Koran, and look forward at death only to a closer intimacy with Him than that which will be enjoyed by those who have not entered on the Path."

CHAPTER VII

THE COSTUMES, MUSICAL INSTRUMENTS, AND SYMBOLIC OBJECTS OF THE DERVISHES

" flutes In Dervish hands at mystic dance,

Whose hopes or fears, loves, joys, or cares,

Are whispered in ecstatic trance."

IzzeT MolLA, The Reedpen's Reply.

" Stone about its waist begirdled, and with iron staff in hand, Trembungly the compass-needle seeketh for the Loved One's Land."

Jam!.

The Dervishes of the various Orders may be easily distinguished from their fellowmen, and also, generally, from each other, by their costumes, and, more particularly, by the shape of their headdresses; and to the latter, as well as to every other article of their clothing, some symbolic meaning, and, in many cases, some legend is attached.

The out-of-door costume of the Mevlevi Order is said to have been adopted by their talented founder Mevlana (Our Lord) Jelalii-'d-Din, as a sign of mourning for his friend and spiritual master, Shemsii-'d-Din (" Sun of the Faith "). It consists of a tall hat called a kulah, of undyed camel's hair felt, in shape like an inverted plantpot. Their Sheikhs, who all claim descent from the family of the Prophet, are, on this account, entitled to wear round their kulah a green turban. The legend attached to this head-dress says that the soul of Mohammed had a previous existence in the Alemi Ervah, or Spirit World, where Allah placed it in a vase of hght of that shape. The lay members of the Order, who do not wear the Dervish dress except when taking part in its ceremonies, often, when in private, lay aside their ordinary fez, or turban, and don the kulah, in ordcr to enjoy the happy influence it is believed to exert on the wearer. When the son of Othman I, Solyman Pasha, asked the blessing of the Mevlevi Grand

Master at Konieh on the expedition he was undertaking against the Byzantine Greeks, that dignitary placed on his head a kulah, and prophesied that " victory should go with him." The prince showed his reverence for the gift by having it covered with silver. So high was the favour which this Order enjoyed under the early Sultans, that their kulah became the state headdress at the Ottoman Court. It was worn, ornamented with gold embroidery, by successive " Commanders of the Faithful," and also, variously decorated, by civil and miutary dignitaries until the beginning of the present century, when " the Reforming Sultan," Mahmoud II, relegated its use to the officers of the Janissary Corps.

The khirkha of the Mevlevi Order is a long, loose, wide-sleeved robe of fawn-coloured cloth for ordinary wear, and of black stuff when used to cover the costume in which they dance. Like the mantles of the Dervishes generally, it is more or less a copy of that beueved to have been worn by the Prophet.

The tennuri, or skirt, is worn only by Mevlevi Dervishes when performing their rehgious exercises. It may be red, yellow, or brown; is made very wide and without gores, and reaches to the feet. The rapid motion of the wearers when spinning round in their mystic dance extends these skirts to their full width, exposing to view the drawers of white linen worn beneath. The upper part of the body is clad in a short jacket of coloured material with tight-fitting sleeves, and round the waist is bound the taybend, a girdle containing in its folds the " Stone of Contentment." This is commemorative of the stones formerly carried by begging Dervishes, who bound them close to their stomachs in order to suppress the pangs of hunger. Three were usually carried, though their wearers confidently believed that Allah would not fail to send relief before the necessity arose for using the full number.

The use of vocal and instrumental music by this Order is said to have been adopted by its founder in order to rouse the lethargic natures of the inhabitants of Riim to a devotional love of Allah through the allurement of sweet sounds addressed to their outward senses. The orchestra of their chief Tekkeh at Konieh is composed of six different instruments, among which are the reedfiute and zither, the rebeck, a kind of violoncello, drums, and tambourines. In the generality of their Tekkehs, however, only zithers, reedflutes, and small hemispherical drums are used. The music of these flutes appears to have a singularly entrancing effect on the Dervishes whose exercises it accompanies. They are lulled and soothed by it to a forgetfulness of the visible world as if they indeed heard in its strains the mystic voices of the spiritual world. In the " Song of the Reed-flute " above quoted, the Dervish poet symbohses under the figure of a Lover sighing for his absent Mistress, the Soul of Man languishing for reunion with the Divine Love. In the Mesnevi of Jelalu-'d-Dm is given the following charmingly poetical account of the origin of the reed-flute's mystic music which recalls the beautiful myth of Orpheus and his lute.

" One day the Prophet privately imparted to Ali the Secrets and Mysteries of the Brethren of Sincerity—evidently the original Brotherhood—with the injunction not to reveal them to anyone. For forty days Ali kept these secrets locked in his breast, but feeling no longer able to contain them, he fled into the desert. Coming upon a well, he stooped as far as possible down its mouth, and to the earth and water divulged, one by one, these mysteries. Some days afterwards a shepherd youth, whose heart had been miraculously enhghtened, perceived a single reed growing up out of the well. He cut it down, drilled holes in it, and, while pasturing his sheep in the neighbourhood, breathed through the flute he had made melodies hke those performed by the Dervish Lovers of Allah. Soon the various Arab tribes heard of the youth's wonderful flute-playing, and came to listen to it, accompanied 1 See p. 52.

by their sheep and camels, which forgot to graze while hearkening. The nomad shepherds wept for joy and delight, and broke forth into transports and ecstasies. The fame of this music at length reached the Prophet, who sent for the youthful musician. When he began to play before them, all the holy disciples of Allah's Messenger were moved to tears; they burst forth into shouts and exclamations of pure bliss, and lost all earthly consciousness. When he had ceased, the Prophet declared that the notes of the shepherd's pipe were the interpretation of the Holy Mysteries which he had confided to the keeping of Ali.

" Thus it is," adds the author, " that, until a man acquires the sincere devotion of the linnet-voiced reedflute, he cannot hear in its dulcet tones the Mysteries of the Brethren of Sincerity, nor reahse the dehghts thereof; for faith is altogether a yearning of the heart and a gratification of the spiritual sense.

"The pangs my love for thee excites, can I to mortal breathe? Ah no! Like All's, some pure fount my sighs, too, must receive. Perchance some reeds may thence upspring its brink to overgrow, And plaintive flutes those reeds become to murmur forth my woe."

The cap, mantle, and girdle of the Bektsshi Order are called by their wearers " The Three Principles," or " Points," and have the following legendary origin. The Angel Gabriel on the occasion of one of his visits to the Prophet, cut his hair, shaved his beard, and then invested him with a cap, mantle, and girdle. This act of service the Angel had previously performed only for Adam and Abraham. Mohammed then proceeded to do for Ali what Gabriel had done for him, and Ah in his turn performed this oihce for the Twelve Imams.

Much symbouc significance is also attached to the Bektashi cap. It is called a Taj, or crown," and is of white felt, shaped like a dome, and divided into four parts by grooves, called " Doors," which allude to the four great stages of the spiritual life. These " Doors" are subdivided by other three grooves into twelve parts, in remembrance of the twelve Imams, and signify also the abandonment of twelve sins. The green or black turban worn round the cap is called the " parable " (Istlva). It signifies the abandonment of the world for the pursuit of high and holy things. As a general rule, the Sheikhs alone wear turbans. They, however, frequently appoint deputies who, as they bear the same honorary title, are also entitled to wear this distinctive head-dress. The cap has, besides, thirteen mystical significations attached to its several parts, among which are its border, circumference, " key," or apex, and decoration. This cap is, spiritually speaking, of two kinds: the " Crown of the Ignorant " (Taj i Jahil), the wearers of which are often to be seen in the bazaars and public streets; and the " Crown of the Perfect " Taj i Kiamil), worn by those who shun, rather than seek, intercourse with the world.

There are also other forms of the Bektashi Ta;, for, according to their saying: "As all the letters of the alphabet grew out of the first one, Alif, so the caps of the various

Orders were derived from the Alifer, or original cap." It is sometimes also called " the Founder" (Pir), and was in earher times inscribed with the text: " All things will perish, save His face, and to Him will all things return." On putting it on, the Dervish recites this invocation:–

" Sign of the glorious name of the Pit of his Order; of Kamber, the groom of Ah; of those who are dead; of the great family of the Imam Riza; permit me to put on this Crown, for I fully believe in its virtues. Great is Allah."

The mantle of the Bektashi Order, though similar in shape, differs from that of the Mevlevi Dervishes in being decorated with twelve lines, or stripes, symbohcal, hke the grooves in their " Crowns," of the Twelve Imams, and is edged with green. Among its mystical attributes are the following, with their meanings as given by the fourth Imam, Jafer-es-Sadik.

Its " True Faith " = to use it as a covering for the faults and folhes of others.

Its Kihleh (point to which the attention is turned, or Mekka) = the Pir.

Its " Ablution " = the cleansing from sin.

Its " Obhgation " = the forsaking of cupidity.

Its " Duty " = Contentment.

Its " Soul " = the keeping of vows.

The eighth Imam.

The different parts of this garment have also their several significations. Its border is symbolical of the condition of a Dervish; its collar, of submission; its exterior signifies " spiritual light," and its interior " secrecy." The collar and edges are embroidered with Arabic words signifying " 0 Friend! " " O Healer! " " O Great One! " etc.

The short tight-sleeved vest worn under the mantle is also decorated with twelve stripes of a colour different from the material, likewise symbolising the twelve Imams.

The girdle worn folded round the waist under the mantle is made from the wool of the sheep sacrificed at the initiation of its owner, and is characterised by several symbohcal names. The Bektashi Dervishes relate that its prototype was worn by Adam, and subsequently by a succession of sixteen Prophets, beginning with Seth, and including Elias, Jesus, and Mohammed. Their legend also says that the one presented to the Prophet by the Angel Gabriel bore the inscription: " There is no God but Allah, Mohammed is His Prophet, and Ali is His Friend." The kamherieh is the rope placed round the neck of the Dervish at his initiation, and subsequently worn by him round his waist. Three knots are tied in it, called respectively the hand-tie, the tongue-tie, and the rein-tie, to remind the wearer of his vows of truth, honesty, and chastity. It is also commemorative of the cord with which Kamber, the groom of the Khalif Ali, was in the habit of tethering his master's horse, "Diildiil," and serves to support a septagonal crystal, or stone, called the Palenky symbolising " the seven heavens and seven earths, seven seas and seven planets," which, according to the Koran, obey Allah's command and worship him by revolving round His holy seat. Another stone, called the " Stone of Submission " (teshem task) is worn suspended round the neck, and attached to it is the following curious legend:–

" Moses, the Servant of God, was in the habit of bathing in the Nile at a spot remote from that used by his fellows for that purpose, in order that they might not observe the radiance that emanated from his body. The evil-minded took advantage of this custom of the Seer to circulate a report that he was leprous, or afflicted with elephantiasis, and for that reason was ashamed to wash with them. But Allah cleared him from the scandal which they had spoken concerning him. One day when Moses was bathing, he laid his clothes on a stone by the riverside. The stone immediately set off at a rapid pace towards Misr (Cairo), followed by the Seer, who, eager in the chase after his garments, found himself amid the Israehtes before he was aware. When he came up with the stone, in his wrath he perforated it with his stick in twelve places. The stone then spake and said, O Moses, I walked by the command of the Lord, and was the cause that thy purity has been witnessed by the people. Moses, being sorry for his unjust behaviour, 1 Koran, Chap, xxxiii.

said, I have perforated thee in twelve places, for which I ask thy forgiveness– A Dervish is forgiven by Dervishes. Well, Moses, rephed the stone, I am satisfied with thy excuses; but now take a cord, and pass it through one of the holes, and keep me till thou requirest a collar of penitence. Moses did as the stone commanded, and suspended it round his neck." " And this," says the Dervish Evhya, " is the origin of the stones generally worn by Dervishes, and also of that put on by penitents, both of which are called sigil tashi. According to the same author, this is the stone that spake to Moses at the rock of Horeb: " O Moses, put me on the ground, and give me twelve blows," upon which twelve streams gushed out of the holes.

Another legend says that the " Stone of Submission " had its origin with Abii Bekr, who, having one day used language which gave offence to the Prophet, repented of his fault, and, to guard against its repetition, hung round his neck a pebble, which he placed in his mouth on entering the mosque.

When putting on for the first time the " Stone of Submission," the Dervish utters this prayer:–

" O Allah, the rites of the Brethren have become my faith; no doubt now exists in my heart. As I hang round my neck the teshem tdsh, I give myself to Thee. In the name of Allah, the Merciful, and the Clement." Then follows the recitation of the 1 This reputed saying of Moses has remained a current expression in the mouth of Dervishes.

chapter of the Koran relative to the striking of the rock by Moses.

A stone of a crescent shape called the mengoosh tdsh is also worn as an earring. It is supposed to represent the shoe of Ah's horse " Diildiil." A Dervish who wears it in only one ear is called a Hassani; one who wears it in both, a Hussaini– these terms referring to the two sons of AH. The wearing of these earrings signifies that the Dervish accepts the words of his spiritual Guide as those of Allah, and that they are the laws that he hangs perpetually over his heart. When he inserts them, he prays: " End of all increase; Ring about the neck of all prosperity; Token of those who are in Paradise; Gift of the Martyr Shah (Hussein)! Cursed be Yezld! " (his murderer).

The post or postaki, the sheepskin mat on which the Dervish sits, has also its attributes. Its head signifies " Submission "; its feet, "Service "; the right side, the " Hand " given to a brother at his initiation; the left, "Honour "; the east, "Secrecy"; the west " Rehgion "; the middle, "Love." It has also, among other symbols, its Law, which means absorption into the Divine Love, when the soul is freed from the body, and wanders away to join other sympathetic spirits.

A curved stick called the chellek is kept in the Bektashi Tekkehs for the chastisement of erring Dervishes. It is commemorative of that used by the Khahf to chastise his groom, Kamber, who thenceforth humbly carried it in his girdle.

9–(2119)

A curiously shaped instrument called the tehher has been mentioned as used by the Bektashis at their ceremonies of initiation, when it is carried by one of the Interpreters," or sponsors. The members of this Order carry also a horn in shape like that of a wild goat, and a two-beaked almsbowl. The former is sounded in the Tekkehs to call the Brethren to their meals and devotions, and is used generally as a signal from one Dervish to another. It appears to be an imitation of that said to be carried by the Angel Gabriel, and is also called by one of the attributes of the Deity–"O Loving"–and a Bektashi carrying it makes use of that exclamation.

The cap of the Riifai, or, as they are commonly termed by Europeans, the " Howling " Dervishes, is very similar in form and material to that worn by the Bektashi Order, and is also called a " Crown." It is of undyed felt, but divided into eight, instead of twelve grooves, each signifying the renunciation of a sin–or what they conceive to be such. The " Crowns " of their Sheikhs are, however, divided into twelve grooves which have the same symbolism as those of the Bektashis, and their turbans are black.

The mantles of the Riifai Order may be of any colour, but are always bordered with green. The reason for this is given in the following somewhat vapid little legend: " The Prophet once, on receiving some good tidings from the Angel Gabriel, started up and turned round so suddenly that his green mantle fell off his shoulders. His disciples A MEVLEVI PLAYER ON THE NEY, OR REED-FLUTE (with his consent, presumably) took possession of the mantle, tore it into shreds, and sewed them round the edges of their own garments. As the Prophet frequently wore a black khirka, the Sheikhs of this Order often follow his example."

The knives, red-hot irons and coals, and other instruments used by the Riifai Order in their extraordinary religious exercises, are called by the symbolic name of Roses." This is evidently connected with the rose-symbolism of the Kadiri Order, whose Pir or founder, Abdul KSdr Ghilani, was, as above mentioned, the uncle and spiritual teacher of the Pir of the Riifai Dervishes.

The Kadiri Rose, embroidered on the " Crowns " of the Brethren of that Order, is to them full of mystic meaning. Tradition says that the Prophet bestowed the name of his " Two Roses " on his grandsons, Hasan and Hussain; and the Sheikhs of 1 Tradition relates that the Prophet, at his death, bequeathed his mantle to the Dervish Sheikh Uwais, referred to on p. 2. It is said to be a long robe of woollen material made with a collar, and wide sleeves reaching to the knee. The charge of this sacred garment has ever since remained in the family of Uwais. Some years ago when the hereditary guardian of this sacred relic happened to be a minor, a Vakil, or deputy, was appointed by the Sultan to discharge this duty. The mantle is enshrined in one of the buildings comprised within the Old Serai at Stamboul, where it is " venerated " by the Sultan and his Court on the occasion of the annual festival of the Khirka Shereef, and also on the occasion of important national events.

2 To speak of wounds as flowers " is a common figure of speech with Eastern poets. Compare, for instance, Gibb, Ottoman Poetry, p. 240.

the Order, who all claim descent from the family of Mohammed, are credited with the possession of peculiar powers in connection with this flower.

According to a legend of this Order, its Pir was directed by Khidhr to proceed to Bagdad and there take up his abode. On arriving at that city Abdul Kadr received from the resident Sheikh a cup filled to the brim with water, which signified that the place was already full of holy men, and that there was consequently no room for him. Replying in the same symbohc language, the Saint miraculously created a rose–it was mid-winter–and placed it in the cup, which did not even then overflow. When this was carried back to the resident Sheikh, he and those with him read the message: " There is yet room in Bagdad for the Kadiri Rose." Marvelung at the miracle, they exclaimed, ' The Sheikh Abdul Kadr is our Rose! " and going out to meet their saintly guest, they conducted him into the city with every mark of respect.

The conventional rose of the Kadiri has eighteen petals arranged in three rings of five, six, and seven respectively, and its colours are yellow, red, white and black. The five petals are symbohcal of the " five virtues " attributed by the Pir of the Order 1 Sulieman Effendi's work on the Mevlad, or Birth of the Prophet, contains the following couplet in reference to Abdul Kadr:–

Whenever he perspired, each drop became a rose. Each drop, as down it rolled, was gathered as a treasure. 8 See above, p. 22.

to the followers of Islam; the six are symbohcal of the six characteristics of faith; and the seven refer to the seven verses of the Fatiha, the first chapter of the Koran, which is also denominated, among other honourable titles, the " Holy Crown," and the Mother of the Koran."

The Hamzavi Order appear to have no distinctive costume, neither do they make use of any mystical symbols in their worship. On their tombstones, however, are sculptured peculiar signs consisting of single and double triangles, with dots above and below the angles, and the " Solomon's Seal " of six points, without the dots.

The Dervish tesbeh, or Rosary, consists of ninety-nine beads, the number of the ' Beautiful names of Allah "; and as a Dervish invokes each one of these in his Zikr, he records it upon his beads. The rosary is also divided into three equal parts, each of which signifies a formula of worship.

The foregoing are, so far as it is possible to ascertain, the chief among the emblematical meanings connected with the costumes worn and the objects used by the various Orders. They, however, by no means exhaust the list. For, to quote again from Evhya Effendi, " a Dervish's dress is covered without and within with a thousand and one symbols which give occasion for a thousand and one questions. He who is capable of answering them all is a Master of the Science of Mysticism, a true Ascetic, and an Ocean of Knowledge."

CHAPTER VIII

THE VARIOUS RELIGIOUS EXERCISES

" Each Saint and Seer a sacred rite has all his own; Yet, as each rite to Allah leads, their rites are one."

Jelalu-'d-Din. The Mesnevi.

" Mystical dance, which yonder starry sphere Of planets, and of fixed, in all her wheels Resembles nearest."

Milton. Paradise Lost, v, 620-2.

The religious exercises of the Dervishes may be said to be, speaking generally, of but two varieties, the Vocative and the Contemplative. The Orders which follow the Vocative form claim descent from the original congregation of the Khalif Ali; and their authority for this mode of worship they profess to find in the Prophet's injunction: " Call loudly and without ceasing on the name of Allah! " given, tradition says, in reply to his nephew's enquiry as to what he ought to do in order to obtain Divine assistance. The Contemplative Orders, who claim descent from the Brotherhood of Abii Bekr, the Prophet's uncle, quote, on the other hand, Mohammed's injunction to him when they were concealed together in a cave during the Fhght, to recite mentally the Zikr, or invocation of the Divine Name. The exercises of many of the leading Orders, however, and especially of those who follow the vocative form of worship, present other, and even more

VARIOUS RELIGIOUS EXERCISES 123 marked dissimilarities. The services of the Mevlevi, Rijfai, and a few of the other Orders are pubhc, and even foreigners, who are rarely admitted into the mosques at the hours of prayer, are courteously welcomed in the Tekkehs of such Orders. The devotions of the rest are performed strictly in private, and do not, indeed, appear to be of a character attractive to outsiders.

The Mevlevi Order is distinguished by its pecuhar dance, which differs entirely from the rehgious exercises of the rest of the Dervishes. The accompaniment to this sacred dance of instrumental and vocal music is said to have been introduced by the founder of the Order, Jelalu-'d-Din; but dancing, or twirling, by Dervishes had evidently a much more ancient origin, as mention of it occurs in the " Thousand Nights and a Night." The number of brethren taking part in the ceremony is usually from fifteen to thirty, including the musicians. When the latter, wearing their tall hats and long cloaks, have taken their places in the gallery, the rest of the fraternity, similarly dressed, their dancing skirts being tucked up and covered by their mantles, enter the Tekkeh barefooted, and seat themselves to the left of the doorway on the strip of carpet that borders the octagonal, or circular central space. The Sheikh, who wears in addition a green turban round his kulah, advances to a small prayer-mat opposite his disciples, and the service begins at once with the Namaz–the devotions performed five times daily by all good Moslems. The Sheikh then invites the brethren to join him in reciting the Fatiha in these words: " Let us chant the Fatiha, glorifying the holy name of Allah, in honour of the blessed religion of the Prophets, but, above all, of Mohammed Mustapha, the greatest, the most august, the most magnificent of all the celestial envoys, and in memory also, of the first four Khalifs (then follows a list of names of the family of the Prophet, the Pir, and other holy men). Let us pray for the constant prosperity of our holy society, for the preservation of the very learned and venerable Chelebi Effendi, our Master and Lord; for the preservation of the Sultan, the very majestic and clement Emperor of the faith of Islam; for the prosperity of the Grand Vizier, and the Sheikh-ul-Islam, and that of all Mohammedan armies, and of all pilgrims to the holy city of Mekka. Let us pray for the repose of the souls of all the Pits and of all the Dervishes of all other Orders; for all good people, for all those who have been distinguished for their good works, their foundations of charitable estabhshments, and their acts of beneficence. Let us also pray for the Moslems of both sexes in the East and the West, for the maintenance of all prosperity, for the prevention of all adversity, for the accomplishment of all salutary vows, and for the success of all praiseworthy enterprises. Let us finally beseech Allah to deign to preserve us in the gift of His grace, and in the fire of Holy Love."

The Dervishes then chant the Fatiha: " Praise 1 The General of the Order.

VARIOUS RELIGIOUS EXERCISES 125 be to Allah, the Lord of all creatures, the Most Merciful, the King of the Day of Judgment. Thee do we worship, and of Thee do we beg assistance. Direct us in the right way, in the way of those to whom Thou hast been gracious, and not of those against whom Thou art incensed, nor of those who go astray." This is followed by a prayer to the Pir asking for his intercession with Allah and the Prophet. The Sheikh then steps off his prayer-mat, and, standing to the right of it, bows low in reverence to the Pir, by whom it is believed to be now occupied. Taking a step forward, he twists himself round, and, standing to the left of the mat, he bows again. He then resumes his former place, and one of the brethren in the orchestra chants a hymn in praise of the Prophet which is followed by a performance by the orchestra.

An elder, called the Sema Z n–who, Hke the Sheikh, retains his cloak all through the ceremony and does not join in the devr, or turning–now leaves his place among the Dervishes and approaches his Superior. Standing with his right great toe crossed over the left, and his arms crossed on his breast, he bows first to the right then to the left of the Sheikh, kisses his hand, and then takes up his position in the centre of the hall. The rest of the brethren, who have in the meantime risen to their feet, taken off their cloaks and let fall their skirts, now advance in single file. Follpwing the example of the Sema Zan, they bow to the right and left of the Sheikh's prayer mat, with crossed toes, arms folded, and hands grasping their shoulders, and then kiss the hand of their Master, who in return bestows a kiss on their kulaks. This done, they immediately begin to turn, balancing themselves on the left foot while maintaining a rotatory motion with the right. The Sheikh meanwhile remains standing with devout mien and downcast eyes. Gradually the arms of the dancers are extended; the right hand is raised with the palm uppermost, and the left lowered with the palm turned downwards. The eyes are closed, and the head inchned on the left shoulder. Mentally reciting the Zikr they whirl round the " Hall of Celestial Sounds." The faces of even the youngest members wear an expression of deep serenity as they revolve to the sound of the flutes and drums, a music which appears to have an entrancing effect on those who understand its mystic language. For the Dervish " Lovers of Allah " it expresses the harmony of His creation in which they circle like the stars of the empyrean, isolated from the world in a rapture of spiritual love and communion with Him.

Some of the younger Der ishes spin very rapidly. At the Mevleh Khaneh at Salonica I used to remark particularly two neophytes, evidently under eighteen years of age, who were extraordinarily proficient in this exercise; but some of the older brethren turned very slowly and feebly. None, however, showed any signs of fatigue or giddiness. When the devr has continued for some ten or fifteen

VARIOUS RELIGIOUS EXERCISES 127 minutes, the Semd Zdn gives the signal for its discontinuance by stamping with one thinly-shod foot on the floor. The Dervishes, as a rule, all stop at the same instant hke the wheels of a machine, and, very curiously, all in a circle with their faces turned towards the Sheikh, though sometimes one or two, more absorbed than the rest in their mystic ecstasy, fail to hear the signal, which has sometimes to be repeated more than once. Crossing their arms on their breasts, and grasping their shoulders, they bow low to their superior, and then, fauing into single file, pass before him with the same reverences as before, and re-commence their gyrations. This exercise is usually repeated a third time, after which the Dervishes resume their seats on the floor, and cover themselves with their mantles. The service concludes with recitations from the Koran, and the customary prayer for the Sultan.

Each Tekkeh has a particular day, or days, in the week for the pubhc performances of the brethren, and, in places like Constantinople, where there are several communities belonging to the same Order, the Dervishes visit and take part in each other's ceremonies. Nothing, however, forbids a Dervish to take part in the rehgious exercises of another Order, save want of the necessary practice and skill. If a Kadiri, for instance, can perform the devr of the Mevlevi Order, he has only to apply to the superintendent of the Tekkeh for a costume and is welcome to enter the hall with the brethren.

Among the Riifai, Kadiri, Khalveti, Bairami,

Gulshani, Ushaki and some other Orders, the devr consists in the Dervishes holding each other by the hand, or pressing closely together, and increasing the movements of their bodies at every step they take in making the round of the hall. A performer may disengage himself from the circle and desist from the devr at any moment he pleases; but those gifted with greater powers of endurance and more enthusiastic temperaments strive by their exertions to excite the rest. These take off their " crowns "– which they hand to the Sheikh–form an inner circle, entwine their arms and press their shoulders together, repeating incessantly Yd Allah! or Yd Hoo! until compelled by sheer exhaustion to desist.

The Rufai Order not only exceed the others in the violence of their exercises, but use also in their frenzy knives, fire, and hot irons. The opening ritual is the same as that of the generahty of the Orders, but the services last longer, and are divided into five distinct ceremonies, some of which are pecuhar to this Order. The Sheikh is seated on a sheepskin mat in front of the kibleh–the niche in the wall which indicates the direction of Mekka– and the service opens with acts of homage performed before him. Four of the elders first approach, embrace each other, and seat themselves two on either side of their superior. The other Dervishes then come forward one by one, with crossed arms and bowed heads. They first salute the name of the Founder engraved on a tablet of stone over the

VARIOUS RELIGIOUS EXERCISES 129 kibleh, pass both their hands over their faces and beards, and, kneehng in turn before the Superior, kiss his hand, and then proceed to their places on the sheepskin mats spread in a horse-shoe design in front of him. All now chant the Tekbir and the Fatiha. This concluded, the Sheikh pronounces the first attribute of the Deity, repeating it incessantly while the disciples respond Allah! Allah! swaying themselves from side to side and placing their hands in turn on various parts of their bodies. One of the elders then commences the second half of the service by chanting a hymn in praise of the Prophet, the Dervishes meanwhile continuing their repetition of the Zikr; now, however, moving their bodies backwards and forwards. After a while they spring to their feet, and stand close together, swaying by a movement of the whole body from side to side, and then again backwards and forwards, all observing an exact rhythm in their exercise, and continuing the ejaculation of Allah! Allah! varied occasionally by that of Ya Hoo! (" O Him! "). They now appear violently agitated, sigh and sob, shed tears, and perspire profusely; their eyes are closed, their faces pale, and their expression and demeanour languid in the extreme.

The third scene commences to the sound of an Ildhi, or mystical song composed by one of the many canonised Sheikhs of this Order. While it is being sung by two of the elders, the most enthusiastic of the brethren places himself in the midst of his fellows, and by his example excites them to a higher pitch of religious fervour. Should a Dervish belonging to another community happen to be present, it is considered an act of courtesy to offer him this office, and should there be several visitors, they perform it in succession. A Mevlevi, however, is not expected to perform any but his own Devr.

In the fourth scene all the Dervishes lay aside their turbans, form a circle with arms and shoulders pressed against each other, and make the circuit of the hall, alternately striking the floor with their feet in unison, and springing up in a body. The two elders continue their chanting, interrupted from time to time by cries of Yd Allah! and Yd Hoo! which increase, when shouted all together, to the extraordinary sound which has gained for them the name of the " Howhng Dervishes. If at any moment they appear about to stop from sheer exhaustion, the Sheikh exhorts them to fresh exertions by placing himself in their midst. The elders follow suit and outdo the rest in physical agitation, exciting their emulation by every means in their power. Two Dervishes now take down from niches in the wall several sharp-pointed iron instruments, and, having heated them red hot in a brazier, present them to the Sheikh. And now commences the final scene.

The Sheikh recites prayers over the instruments, invokes the name of the Pir, breathes upon them, raises them to his hps, and then presents them to his disciples. These devotees, excited by their previous exercises, are now in the state of rehgious

I–(w h-l

Q H

VARIOUS RELIGIOUS EXERCISES 131 delirium called hal. Some eagerly seize the hot irons, regard them fondly, plunge them into their flesh, lick them, or hold them in their mouths; and all without evincing any sign of pain, but rather as if intoxicated by the perfume of the " Rose of Bagdad," of which they are said to be mystically symbolical. Others seize daggers from their resting-places on the walls, or hot coals from the brazier, with which they cut or burn their flesh. Some fall, overcome by their excitement, into the arms of their brethren; and all finally sink, exhausted and unconscious, on the floor. The Sheikh presently walks among them, whispers in their ears a mystical word that recalls them to consciousness, breathes upon them, and anoints their wounds with his saliva. It is said, and indeed commonly believed by the Mohammedan spectators, that all traces of their hurts disappear within twenty-four hours. A Riifai legend says that their founder, Ahmed Said Rufai, having on one occasion put his legs in a pan of live coals, his burns were immediately healed by the nefs (breath) and saliva of his uncle, Abdul Kadr Ghilani, who at the same time endowed with his healing power the Riifai Pir.

The Devy of the Sadi Order is similar to that just described, but leads to no self-mutilations. It consists chiefly of violent changes of attitude and physical agitation, continued until the devotees finally fall exhausted and unconscious.

The Kadiris, after reciting the Fatiha already 1 See above, p. 119.

described, take each other by the shoulders and turn in a circle round the hall of their Tekkeh. This variety of the devr was not originated by the founder of the Order, but was adopted at the instance of one of its most eminent Sheikhs.

Among the " contemplative" Dervishes the Bektashis are the most numerous. Their devotions, after the customary recitations, are conducted in silence, a form of worship known as the Hiffl.

The service of the Nakshibendi Order consists of one prayer called the Iklah, repeated a thousand and one times. This number of pebbles is distributed among the brethren who are seated in a circle on the floor; and, as each one completes the mental recitation of an Iklah, he lays down before him a pebble until the whole number are deposited within the circle.

The Hamzavis, or as they are also called, Melami-youns, appear to have in former centuries maintained great secrecy with regard to their rehgious rites—a fact that not unnaturally gave rise to suspicions of their orthodoxy. They were accused of belonging to the Order of Freemasons, and, as related in a subsequent chapter, were subjected to active persecution. To judge, however, from their Litany, they appear to be a singularly pious sect, and they enjoy the reputation of being most conscientious in all their dealings, hving only for

1 The term Fermason = " Freemason," is, among orthodox Moslems, synonymous with " infidel.

2 Below, p. 186.

VARIOUS RELIGIOUS EXERCISES 133 their doctrines, regardless of the things of this world.

The following account of their rites and principles from the writings of Abdul Baki, a Dervish of the Order, is quoted from Mr. Brown's The Dervishes:–

" Whenever those who follow in this path, and who love the unique God, to the number of two or three, or more, are about to meet together and join in the tevheed and the zikyy and their hearts are occupied with their worldly affairs, they should, on their way to the place of meeting, employ their minds with thoughts of God, in all sincerity and purity, and also beg their Pir to lend them his spiritual aid, so that when they reach the place of meeting they may all, small and great, with humihty and contrition, embrace the hand of each other, and devoutly join in the contemplation of the Deity, and turn their faces towards the Grace of the All-Just, the ever rising Love of Allah, without harbouring in the tongue, in the mind, or otherwise, any thoughts respecting worldly concerns, but, with perfect hearts and active spirits, take part in these pious ceremonies.

" They must next offer up those prayers which are conformable with the rules of the Order, seat themselves, and, if there be among them anyone possessing a pleasing voice, let him read aloud ten verses of the great Koran, and interest the congregation with some account of the Prophets and Saints, or 1 P. 182.

10–(3119) even of the Deity. No one must feel concern about his worldly affairs, but the remarks of all must relate to the Love of Allah, or tend to pious fervour. No one not belonging to the Order must be admitted, for, should any such be present, the pecuhar gift of God (Faiz Ullah) will not be vouchsafed."

The aim of the Nakshibendi Order, in the performance of their zikr, is to detach the senses completely from worldly surroundings. The Sheikh and his disciples sit facing each other, the former mentally reciting the invocation, while each of the brethren endeavours to keep his attention fixed by placing his heart in imagination in view of that of his Master, closes his eyes and hps, presses his tongue against the roof of his mouth, and so regulates his breathing that between each respiration he can mentally repeat three times the zikr.

As already mentioned, the Order of the Nakshibendi was a revival of the original fraternity of Abu Bekr which, by the successful estabhshment of other Orders, had become extinct. The Brotherhood meet once a week, generally on a Thursday at sunset, the hour of the fifth Namdz or daily prayer. In each city, suburb, or quarter (mahalldh) the members of this religious society assemble at the houses of their respective Sheikhs, where, seated round the room on the divan, they perform their devotions. The Superior, or one of the fraternity, chants the prayers, and the assembly responds Hoof or Allah! In some cities, how ever, this 1 Above, p. 17.

VARIOUS RELIGIOUS EXERCISES 135

Order possesses special Tekkehs in which their services are held; and in these cases their Sheikh is distinguished from his congregation by a turban similar to that worn by the Imams who officiate in the mosques.

CHAPTER IX

SURVIVALS OF PAGANISM

" The talisman of magic might, Hid in some ruin's lonely site, Emerges from its ancient night At the mild glance of Dervishes."

Hafiz.

Considering that the existence of magic and witchcraft, and the power of the " Evil Eye " are stated as absolute facts in the Koran, it is not surprising that in Mohammedan countries superstitious behefs and practices play so great a part in the social life of the people. For to deny the existence of magicians and enchantments would be tantamount to denying the authenticity of the Holy Book; and a devout Moslem, even if sufficiently enhghtened to discredit the popular superstitions that meet him at every turn, is constrained to admit that magic was practised on the very person of the Prophet. The words made use of as counter-spells, and exorcisms are, indeed, taken chiefly from the two chapters of the Koran relating to magic and malevolence, and beginning:–

" Say, I fly for refuge unto the Lord of the Daybreak, that he may deliver me from the mischief of those things which He hath created, and from the mischief of the night when it cometh on, and from the mischief of women blowing on knots, and from the mischief of the envious when he envieth," etc.

Commentators on the Koran relate that the reason for the revelation of these chapters was that a Jew named Lobeid, had, with the assistance of his daughters, bewitched Mohammed by tying eleven knots in a cord which they hid in a well. The Prophet falhng ill in consequence, this chapter and that following it were revealed; and the Angel Gabriel acquainted him with the use he was to make of them, and told him where the cord was hidden. The Khalif Ali fetched the cord, and the Prophet repeated over it these two chapters; at every verse a knot was loosed, till, on finishing the last words, he was entirely freed from the charm.

In the chapter on Convents and Shrines I have described a somewhat similar operation performed by a Mevlevi Dervish at the tomb of St. Dimitri. In this case, however, the knots were evidently made with the object of " t3 ng up " sickness and other ills.

The ignorant among the Moslems of Turkey, in

Koran, Surah cxiii, 2 In a note to this chapter in his translation Mr. Sale says that the words " blowing on knots " refer to " witches who used to tie knots and to blow upon them, uttering at the same time certain magical words over them in order to work on or debilitate the person they had a mind to injure." In the same note it is stated that " this was a common practice in former days—what they call in France nouev Veguillette—and the knots which the wizards in the northern parts tie when they sell mariners a wind are relics of the same superstition."

common, it must be admitted, with the native Christians and Jews, attribute the majority of the ills the flesh is heir to, and also misfortunes generally, to the influence of magic; and, consequently, have recourse to the same mysterious agency for their cure. By the populace the Dervishes are held to be experts in the magic of the old Paganism, belief in which is thus sanctioned by their Holy Book. They are, indeed, credited with the faculty not only of heahng mental and bodily diseases, but also of counteracting the effects of witchcraft and sorcery, of interpreting dreams, recovering lost or stolen property, and even of restoring to wives the waning affection of their husbands. When anyone falls ill, the women of the family—for it need hardly be said that the firmest behevers in this mode of spiritual cure are of the female sex—send for some saintly Sheikh to remove the spell which has caused the ailment, or, at least, to counteract its influence. This holy man, whose breath, sanctified by the constant repetition of the Divine Name (Zikr), has acquired a supernaturally heahng power, breathes on the head and afflicted parts of the patient, laying at the same time his hands upon him. This concluded, he produces a tiny scroll of paper inscribed with some sacred words, or a passage from the Koran, which he orders to be either swallowed by the sufferer, soaked in water and the hquid drunk, or worn on the person for a stated number of days. It is recorded in the Mesnevi that Jelalu-'d-Din made use of this remedy to cure a disciple suffering from intermittent fever. The potion was accompanied by the following supplication in which the malady is personahsed and addressed by a propitiatory title:—

" O Mother of the Sleek One! If thou hast beueued in Allah, the Most High, make not the head to ache, pollute not the throat, devour not the flesh, drink not the blood, and depart thou out of, betaking thyself to one who attributes to Allah partners of other false gods. And I testify that there is no god but God, and that Mohammed is His Servant and Apostle."

Among other exorcisms, the use of which is said to have originated at the time of Mohammed, it is related by the historian, Ahmet Effendi, that, in the tenth year of the Hegira, the Khahf Ah being about to march against the province of Yemen, the army of which far outnumbered his own, expressed some anxiety as to the success of the expedition. To reanimate the courage of his nephew, the Prophet put his own turban on the head of Ali, and pressed his hands on his breast, saying, O Allah, purify his tongue, strengthen his heart, and direct his mind! " Religious tradition has exaggerated the importance of these words until they have come to be considered the source from which the exorcising 1 The smallpox is similarly designated by the Greeks " the Blessing," and by the Dyaks of Borneo " the Chief." The Greeks have many similar exorcisms. See Polites,

At Ac evetat Kara rods xvoovs tov E r VikOv Aaoc, in the Aexrlou rrjs Ifftopikris Kal E6vo oyikfjs Eraipias Vol. I. One of these has been given in my Greek Folk-poesy, Vol. II.

Sheikhs derive the virtue and efficacy of their spiritual remedies.

Cabahstic talismans prepared by Dervishes are also in great request as preventives against, as well as cures for, real and imaginary calamities, and are constantly worn attached to the head-dress, or hung round the neck. The efficacy of the scrolls just described, which are called by the various names of nushka, yafta, and hammdil, can only be rehed upon, according to the Sheikhs who prescribe them, when administered by their own hands. But whatever the success of these remedies may be in individual cases, nothing can shake popular belief in their general efficacy. If the patient is not benefited by them, the fault naturally Hes in his want of faith, or in the neglect of some other condition. The holy man, in any case, receives an honorarium for his services, either in coin or in kind; but if a speedy cure is the result of his ministrations, his reward will be large in proportion.

The Dervishes, in common with all Orientals, attach great sacredness to the thirty-four letters of the Arabic Alphabet, and assign to each a numerical value. Of this mode of thinking we have a familiar illustration in the Apocalyptic puzzle of the name of the seven-headed beast which is the number of a man; and his number is six hundred and three score and six," a puzzle of which the true solution has been shown to be ipwv Kalaap, the value of which letters, transcribed in Hebrew, is iq. Most

Revxiii, 18.

persistent, too, have been the superstitious notions with regard to numbers. We find that in 1666, the Jews, not only in the East, but in many parts of Europe, were so confident of the appearance of the Messiah that the Jewish imposter, Shabathai Shevi, found himself surrounded by disciples in every town in which he announced his Messiahship. And that, even in England at the present day, belief in the " magic of figures is not extinct is evident from a paragraph which appeared in a London newspaper at the beginning of 1888, recording the eventful character to this country of former years whose three final figures were ahke, and suggesting that the same being the fact in 1888 " is itself portentous. The numerical values of the Arabic alphabet are made use of to draw up a class of tahsmans of a mystical and cabalistic character by means of what the Dervishes call the " Science of Calculation." Chronograms are written according to the same system, and in many of the inscriptions on public edifices, the last line, though written in the same character as the rest, and expressing in connection with them some poetical idea, will be found, on calculation, to give also the date of its composition. Eminent Dervishes were often commanded by the early Sultans to compose such inscriptions as " talismans " for the gateways of conquered towns, or newly-erected public buildings. Hadji Bektash is said to have composed many of these inscriptions, and, very curiously, the letters forming his name 1 Pall Mall Gazette, Jan. 5, 1888.

give at the same time the date of the foundation of his Order.

Tahsmanic charms are also often composed, among other methods, of cabahstic calculations based on the numerical value of the letters composing the name of the person interested. In a divination for the purpose of fortune-telling, these values are multiphed and divided, and their cubes and squares added and subtracted according to some conventional formula, to obtain a result, odd or even. If even, it is considered lucky; if odd, the reverse.

The idea of the sacred and mysterious character of letters has also given rise to a belief that each one has its special attendant Djin appointed by Allah to wait upon it, and that these Djins may be invoked either severally or collectively. In order to secure the invisible presence of these " Slaves of the Letter," the calculations must be drawn up on certain days and hours, and at certain pei; iods of the moon and positions of the stars. Such cabalistic figures are also frequently engraved on stones brought from the holy cities of Mekka, Medina, or Damascus, or from the neighbourhood of the tombs of holy men such as Hadji Bektash, or Hadji Bairam. Sometimes, however, these amulets are inscribed with a verse from the Koran, or an invocation addressed to the Prophet or the Khahf Ah. When a charm is concocted for the purpose of inspiring someone with the tender passion, the Djins invoked by it are believed to meet in council in order to

A WANDERING DERVISH devise a series of influences which will compel the person aimed at to obey them. The only antidote against such a charm is to draw up one that will ensure another assembly of Djtns who will either overcome the first, or compel them to agree to a compromise, and so release the victim from their influence. Some of the talismans purchased from these Dervish magicians are credited with the power of procuring the visits of beneficent Djins who cure the suffering in body, ease the troubled in mmd, and grant the desires of the person invoking their aid. Other charms are beheved to influence dreams when placed under the pillow of one asleep.

The four elements are also credited with the possession of twenty-eight letters having numerical values ranging from one to a thousand. They are divided into four classes of seven each, and to each class is attributed a " temperament " according to the nature of the element its letters represent. To the letters representing water is given the predominance over all the others, as, in accordance with the Mohammedan account of the creation, water was the original element, and from it the other three were created. Calculations are made to discover which of the four elements exists in too large a proportion in the system of a suffering person; and when this has been discovered, a charm (nushka) is drawn up, which, swallowed or worn next to the skin, will enable the patient to get rid of the superabundant element.

1 Sales' Koran. Chap, xli, p. 356, n.

The Dervishes are also often had recourse to for the recovery of lost or stolen property. Sheikh AH, the head of the Bektashi fraternity at Salonica before mentioned, enjoyed a great reputation for success in this particular line of his profession. His mode of procedure was to ascertain the names of all the persons who had visited a house where any such loss had been sustained and visit each in turn. While gossiping about the event he would let drop a hint that the guilty person would be made the object of some magical charm if he did not at once restore the property to its owner; and, superstitious fear getting the better of cupidity, the lost article would usually be recovered as mysteriously as it had disappeared. The skill of this Dervish as an interpreter of dreams was also said to rival that of a famous Turkish witch in the city. I happened on the occasion of one of his visits to have had my sleep disturbed on the previous night by a dream of green snakes, and took the opportunity of asking for his explanation of it. Divining, no doubt, that I was not of a credulous or superstitious turn of mind, he merely replied, with a shrug of the shoulders and a graceful gesture of the hands, "Eyei olsoun! " (May it be good).

Dervishes figure not infrequently in Oriental folk-tales, both Moslem and Christian. Everyone is acquainted with the " One-eyed Kalender " of the Thousand Nights and a Night, though few, perhaps, recognise in the bearer of that appellation a wandering
Above, p. 40.

Dervish. In Greek folk-tale, Dervishes are often credited with the possession of magical objects such as cups that are instantly filled with whatever the owner may desire; knives that slay man or beast at his command; reed-flutes, the sound of which brings the dead to life; turbans of invisibility, etc., etc. Stories are also current of secret hoards of wealth wrested by Dervish Sheikhs, deeply versed in magic, from the guardianship of Djins who had possessed them from time immemorial in their subterranean palaces.

Compare, for instance, Greek Folk-poesy, "The Story of the Soothsayer," Vol. II, p. 230.

CHAPTER X

THE ACTS OF THE ADEPTS

" A Saint is aware of every thought of the King's heart, and of every secret on earth or in heaven."– Saying of Jelalu-'d-D! n.

As mentioned in previous chapters, the mental and physical condition necessary for the manifestation of their abnormal powers is termed by the Dervishes Hal, a word simply signifying ' state." There appear, however, to be two distinct descriptions of Hal, induced by methods of a totally opposite character, and resulting in powers which differ in a corresponding degree.

The first appears to be of a merely temporary nature, and is found only among certain Orders such as the Rufai " Howling Dervishes ") during their religious exercises performed collectively in the hall of their Tekkeh. As has been seen in the chapter on the Religious Exercises, the devotees, by a contagious emulation, work themselves and each other into an abnormal state of agitation, both mental and physical, during which they inflict upon themselves injuries which, under ordinary conditions, would be dangerous, if not fatal, but which, when inflicted while they are in this strange state of excitement, are, in many cases, not even followed by the loss of a drop of blood, and are mysteriously and speedily healed by the breath and spittle of the Sheikh. That mental states are contagious we have, I think, abundant evidence in cases of panic, when persons, without having the faintest idea of the cause, will excitedly join in the general rush; and also in so-called Christian " Revivals "–instances of which are, perhaps, more common in America than elsewhere, and especially among the excitable negro population, when, during an enthusiastic camp meeting," many persons become perfectly frenzied with religious excitement.

The dance Devr) of the Mevlevi Dervishes also produces a species of Hal. It would indeed be difficult to account otherwise for the ability of some twenty men and youths to spin round with closed eyes and outstretched arms within a limited circle for the space of from ten to fifteen minutes without either coming into couision with each other, or showing any signs of giddiness–a scarcely possible feat under ordinary conditions.

The second description of Hal, which appears to be permanent, or, at least, assumable at will, is attained only by those Dervishes who, through long and fervent contemplation of the Deity, have arrived at the Fourth, or highest degree, that of " Union with Allah." Sheikhs and Dervishes of superior grade, belonging to all Orders, whether

A curious illustration of this occurred a few years ago in Ottawa, where a series of revivalist services resulted, according to the Montreal Star, in the " conversion " of the Premier of the Dominion and his lady, though his name " has so long been the synonym of iniquity in many worthy minds."

Vocative or Contemplative, are equally credited with ability to acquire this degree of sanctity; and on attaining it they become endowed with various spiritual and superhuman powers. Among these may be named what is termed the " Power of the Will," thought-reading, the gift of prophecy, knowledge of what is happening afar off, and power to influence the event, as also ability to appear in person at great distances for the help of friends or the confusion of enemies, and miracle-working generally. These wonderful gifts can, it is beheved, be transmitted by a Sheikh, with his mantle of office, to the disciple who shall prove himself by his rapid advance on the Mystic Path to be a worthy recipient of them, even as Elijah bestowed his mantle on Elisha and endowed him with his own miraculous powers. Instances of the exercise of the Power of the Will are to be found in the biography of every Dervish of renown. In some cases the subject is conscious of the influence under which he is acting, in others he is quite unaware of it, as in the following incident related by the learned Siifi, Mohammed Baha-'d-Din, of his spiritual Master:–

" In my youth I was ever with Our Lord (Mevlana) Saed ed Din of Kashgar at Hereed. It happened one day, as we were walking out together, that we came upon a number of the people of the place who were engaged in the exercise of wrestling. We agreed together to aid one of the wrestlers so that he might throw his opponent, and afterwards to change our design in favour of the discomfited one.

THE ACTS OF THE ADEPTS 149

So we stopped as if to look on, and as we looked, gave the full influence of our united wills to one individual, and he was immediately able to vanquish the other. Each person we chose in turn vanquished his opponent, and the power of our wills was thus clearly manifested."

This Sheikh also took an active part in the wars of his time between the Sultans of Bokhara and Samarcand; and by means of his wonderful powers is held to have greatly influenced their history. The monarch who took the precaution of securing his goodwill was invariably victorious; while those who disdained his assistance met with loss and disaster; and many persons who had wronged the Sheikh or his friends in the troubled times in which he lived felt the weight of his spiritual displeasure. Some even fell sick and died, or recovered only after making full confession and restitution, and obtaining his pardon and intercession with Allah on their behalf. It was said that he could hold converse vith his disciples and friends at a great distance, and their appeals to him were always heard and answered.

Over the minds of his followers Sheikh Saed-'d-Din is said to have exercised a peculiar power. He could influence them in such a way as to throw them at will into a species of trance during which they could remember no single event of their past lives, nor anything they had previously learnt; and in this state they would remain until their Master 1 J. P. Brown, The Dervishes. II–(2119) chose to restore to them the possession of their ordinary faculties. This Power of the Will would appear to be but a kind of mesmeric influence, intensified, perhaps, by the complete mental subordination of a disciple to his spiritual guide. "Let your Murshid be always present to your mind, whatever you are doing or saying," is a primary obligation. And when we consider that, in addition to this state of constant mental subjection, the body of the Murid is enfeebled by fasting and his mind fatigued by long vigils and protracted devotions, while his imagination is at the same time fully impressed with the belief that his Superior is really in possession of such powers, it is not difficult to understand that a remarkable ascendancy can be obtained by a Sheikh over his disciples. Nothing indeed could be better adapted to induce susceptibility to hypnotic influences than the discipline to which a Dervish is subjected during his novitiate. And having felt in his own person the potency of the spell of his Murshid, he will easily be led to credit him with the faculty of similarly influencing others.

Not individuals only, however, but crowds have been known to be affected in this way by eminent Dervishes; and according to Moslem legend, even opposing armies have been caused to desist from hostilities, completely subdued by the pacificatory spell thrown over them by some " Man of Peace," who has also compelled their leaders to sign treaties drawn up by himself. The writings of the Sufis THE ACTS OF THE ADEPTS 151 teem with traditions and anecdotes recording the marvellous spiritual attainments of those Higher Mystics, and of the resulting abnormal powers exercised by them. Some of these biographies have been translated into European languages, but of others fragments only are available.

Many strange stories are related of Abdul Kadr of Ghilan, already mentioned as the founder of the Kadiri Order. The poet Sadi records in his " Gulistdn" that when visiting the sanctuary of the Kaaba, the great Sheikh laid his face on the pebbled pavement and prayed: " O Lord! pardon me; but if I am deserving of punishment, raise me up at the resurrection blind, that I may not be ashamed in the sight of the righteous." And Sir John Malcolm gives the following legend, translated by him from a Persian MS., concerning this famous Sheikh: His mother declared that when he was at the breast, he never tasted milk (? from sunrise to sunset) during the holy month of

Ramazan; and in one of his works he gives this account of himself: The day before the feast of Araf, I went out into the fields and laid hold of the tail of a cow, which turned round and exclaimed, " 0 Abdul Kadr, am I not that which thou hast created me? " I returned home and mounted to the terrace of my house: I saw all the pilgrims standing at the mountain of Araf (it at Mekka. I went and told my mother that I must dedicate myself to God: I wished to proceed to Bagdad to obtain knowledge. I informed her of what I had seen, and she wept. Then, taking out eighty deenars, she told me that, as I had a brother, half of that was all my inheritance. She made me swear when she gave it to me, never to tell a lie; and then bade me farewell, exclaiming, "Go, my son, I give thee to God. We shall not meet again until the Day of Judgment! " I went on well till I came to Hamadan, when our Kaffilah (caravan) was plundered by forty horsemen. One fellow asked me what I had got. ' Forty deenars I said, " are sewed under my garment." The fellow laughed, thinking, no doubt, I was joking him. 'What have you got? asked another. I gave him the same answer. When they were dividing the spoil, I was called to an eminence where their chief stood. " What property have you, my Httle fellow? " said he. 'I have told two of your people already," I rephed, that I have forty deenars sewed up carefully in my clothes." He desired them to be ripped open, and found my money. " And how came you," he asked with surprise, ' to declare so openly what has been so carefully hidden?" Because," I replied, "I will not be false to my mother whom I have promised that I will never tell a lie." ' Child," said the robber, " hast thou such a sense of thy duty to thy mother at thy years; and am I insensible, at my age, of the duty I owe my God? Give me thy hand, innocent boy," he continued, that I may swear repentance on it." He did so. His followers were all alike touched with the scene. ' Thou hast been our leader in guilt," said they to the chief, " be the

CITY GATE CALLED THE MEVLEVI-HANE, STAMBOUL

THE ACTS OF THE ADEPTS 153 same in the path of virtue," and instantly at his order they made restitution of their spoil, and vowed repentance on my hand. "

Abdul Kadr arrived in Bagdad about 1085, and, consequently, when this event happened, he must have been about seventeen years of age. He does not, however, appear to have begun his public lectures until he had reached his fiftieth year. Not only Sufi writers, but eminent Sunni, or orthodox Moslem authorities, record many of his miracles. God granted all his requests, and the Divine vengeance fell on all those who wronged him. He himself gives the following account of the fast he underwent during his probation:– I was eleven years in a tower, and when there I vowed to God that I would neither eat nor drink until some one compelled me to do so. I maintained my fast for forty days, after which a person brought me a little meat, put it before me, and went away. My life was nearly springing out of me at the sight of the victuals, but I refrained; and I heard a voice from within me call out, I am hungry, I am hungry! At that moment Sheikh Abu Seyyid Mukzoomi (a celebrated Siifi) passed, and, hearing the voice, exclaimed, What is that? ' It is my mortal part, I replied, but the soul is yet firm, and awaits the result. ' Come to my house, he said, and went away. I resolved, however, to fulfil my vow, and remained where I was; but Ehas 1 Hist, of Persia. Vol. II, p. 286, n. See above, p. 22.

came and told me to follow the Seyyid, whom I found at his door awaiting me. You would not comply with my wish, said he, until it was enforced by Elias. After this he gave me meat and drink in plenty, and then invested me with a khirka (mantle) and I became his confirmed friend and companion."

Many and wonderful are the legends which have gathered round the name of the great mystic poet, Jelalu-'d-Din. The Acts of the Adepts, compiled by Efiaki in the fourteenth century, contains some hundreds of anecdotes concerning Jelal, his family, friends, and followers, most of which are narratives of supernatural actions performed by living or dead Dervishes, male or female, or of some remarkable event connected with them.

Baha-'d-Din Veled, the father of Jelalu-'d-Din, was hardly less famous among the Mystics of the thirteenth century than was his illustrious son; and besides being closely related to the reigning dynasty of Khorassan, was able to trace his descent to Abii Bekr, the Commander of the Faithful," and uncle of the Prophet. In virtue of his learning and mystic piety, Baha-'d-Din was held in such high estimation by the inhabitants of the capital, Balkh, as to excite the jealous animosity of the Sultan's courtiers, who accused him of aspiring to the throne. He accordingly quitted the city with a following of about forty souls, after delivering in the great mosque a public address in which he foretold the 1 Malcolm, Hist, of Persia, Vol. II, p. 286, n.

THE ACTS OF THE ADEPTS 155 advent of the Moguls and the subversion of the country. Arrived at Bagdad, he was received with great honour by the Khahf, but refused the costly gifts he would have bestowed upon him. Preaching in the mosque, he dared to reprove the monarch to his face for his evil course of life, and foretold that he would be slain by the Moguls under circumstances of great ignominy and cruelty. During Baha-'d-Din's sojourn at Bagdad news came of the conquest of Balkh; he again set out on his travels, and, after various wanderings, was finally invited to Konieh by the Seljuk Sultan, Ala-'d-Din, who had made that city his capital. Here Baha-'d-Din was warmly welcomed and liberally entertained by this prince, under whose auspices he established a college, and from whom he received the honourable title of " Sultan of Learned Men " (Sultan l-Ulemd).

Numerous stories are related of the wonderful spiritual gifts possessed by this illustrious Teacher, and of the great influence he exercised over others, not only during his lifetime, but also after death. One of these relates that when Sultan Alau-'d-Din had fortified Konieh, he invited Baha Veled to mount to the terraced roof of the palace, thence to survey the walls and towers. After this inspection Baha remarked to the Sultan, "Against torrents, and against the horsemen of the enemy, thou hast raised a goodly defence. But what protection hast thou built against those unseen arrows, the sighs and moans of the oppressed, which overleap a thousand walls and sweep whole worlds to destruction? Go to, now! strive to acquire the blessings of thy subjects. These are a stronghold compared to which the walls and turrets of the strongest castles are as nothing."

Another anecdote says that shortly after the death of Baha-'d-Din, the Sultan of Kharism, Jelalii-'d-Din Shah, arrived on the borders of Asia Minor with a great army. On hearing this alarming news, the Sultan of Konieh went to pray at the tomb of the deceased Sheikh, and then prepared to meet the enemy who were encamped in the neighbourhood of Erzeriim. Disguising himself, he set out with a few followers to reconnoitre, and actually entered the enemy's camp. At midnight the sainted Sheikh appeared to him in a dream and warned him to fly. The Sultan awoke, but attaching no importance to the warning, went to sleep again. The Saint now appeared a second time. Ala-'d-Din saw himself seated on his throne, and the Saint approaching him smote him on the breast with his staff, saying angrily, "Why sleepest thou? Arise! " So the Sultan arose, got together his people and horses, and stole from the camp. Not long afterwards the two armies engaged; the Sultan of Konieh came off victorious; and in all subsequent difhculties had recourse to the powerful aid of the Saint whom he had in life honoured and befriended.

Jelalii-'d-Din, who had studied under the most eminent teachers of Aleppo and Damascus, succeeded

Acts of the Adepts, Redhouse's translation, p. 10.

THE ACTS OF THE ADEPTS 157 his father as Director of the College at Konieh, and also in the title of Sultan of Learned Men." The high reputation for piety and learning that the young scholar had already acquired gained for him the devotion of his father's disciples; and in addition to these he soon gathered around him four hundred enthusiastic students by whom he was designated Mevldna (Our Lord), a title from which, as above mentioned, the Order founded by him took its name. Eflaki relates the following incident as illustrative of the close friendship and devotion to each other of these Siifi Saints. An emdnent Sheikh, the Seyyid Burha-nu-'d Din had been a pupil of BSha-'d-Din during his residence at Balkh. On his master's departure from that city, the Seyyid went to Termiz, and, after living some time there as a recluse, he began to lecture publicly. During one of his discourses he suddenly stopped and cried out in a tone of anguish, accompanied by floods of tears: Alas! my Master has passed away from this Tabernacle of Dust to the Abode of Sincerity 1 " His words and the time of their utterance were noted down, and were subsequently found to correspond exactly with the moment of Baha Veled's death. When the disciples at Termiz had mourned forty days for the great Teacher, the Seyyid said to them, The son of my master, Jelalu-'d-Din Mohammed, is left alone and is wishing to see me.

1 This Saint, says Eflaki, was popularly known as Sirr-Dan, "The Confidant," a title signifying " one acquainted with secrets or mysteries."

I must go to the land of Rum, and deliver over to him the trust which my Teacher confided to my safe keeping

On arriving at Konieh, the Seyyid was so much delighted with the discourse of Jelal, that he kissed the soles of his feet, exclaiming, ' A hundred fold hast thou surpassed thy father in all knowledge of the Humanities; but he was versed also in that spiritual knowledge which is attained only through silent contemplation and through ecstasy. From this day forward my aim shall be to instruct thee in that knowledge–the knowledge possessed by the Prophets and Saints and which we term The Science of Divine Intuition. This is the science spoken of by Allah: We have taught him a science from within Us. This knowledge did I acquire from my Teacher; do thou receive it from me, and thus become the heir of thy father in things spiritual as well as in things temporal." Jelsl took the Seyyid to his College, and for nine years was his pupil in mystic lore.

The following story is told of Jelal's student days. While he was pursuing his studies at Aleppo, the superior treatment he received from the professor roused the

jealousy of some of his fellow students, who complained to the governor that Jelal was immoral, as he was in the habit of quitting his cell at midnight for some unknown purpose. The governor resolved to see and judge for himself;
Koran xviii, 64.
2 Acts of the Adepts, pp. 14-15.
he therefore hid himself in the college porter's lodge.
At midnight Jelsl came forth, and went straight to the locked gate of the college, watched by the governor. The gate flew open; and Jelal, followed at a distance by the governor, went through the streets to the locked city gate. This, too, opened of itself; and again both passed through. They went on, and came to the tomb of Abraham (at Hebron, about 350 miles distant). There a domed edifice was seen, filled with a large company of forms in green raiment, who came forth to meet Jelal, and conducted him into the building. The governor hereupon lost his senses through fright, and did not recover until after the sun had risen. He could now see neither edifice nor human being. He wandered about on a trackless waste for three days and nights, and at length sank under his sufferings.
Meanwhile the porter of the college had given intelligence of the governor's pursuit after Jelal. When his officers found that he did not return, they sent a company of soldiers to seek him. These, on the second day, were met by Jelal, who told them where they would find their master. Late on the next day they came up with the governor, found him nearly dead, and brought him home. This dignitary was so impressed by the event that he became a sincere admirer and devoted disciple of Jelal. 1
J Acts of ths Adepts, p. 21.
The two following anecdotes also illustrate the faculty ascribed to the higher Mystics of transporting themselves at will to great distances.
A certain rich merchant of Konieh, a disciple, as was also his wife, of Jelal, went to Mekka one year for the pilgrimage. On the day when the victims are slaughtered, the lady had a dish of sweetmeat prepared, and sent some of it in a china bowl to Jelal, to be eaten at dinner. She made the request that, when he partook of the food, he would favour her absent husband with his remembrance, his prayers, and his blessing. Jelal invited his disciples to the feast, and all ate of the lady's sweetmeat to repletion. But the bowl still remained full. Jelal then said, "Oh, he, too, must partake of it." He took the bowl, ascended to the terraced roof of the college with it, returning immediately empty handed. His friends asked him what he had done with the bowl and the food. I have handed them," said Jelal, to the lady's husband, whose property they are." The company were puzzled by his words and conduct. In due course of time, when the pilgrims returned to Konieh, out of the baggage of the merchant the china bowl was produced, and sent in to the astonished lady, who enquired of her husband how he had become possessed of that identical dish. He replied, "Ah! I am also at a loss to know how it happened. But on the eve of 1 The Qurban Bairam, or annual sacrifice, which takes place while the pilgrims are at Mekka.
2 This is a common custom in the East.
THE ACTS OF THE ADEPTS 161 the slaughter of the victims, I was seated in my tent, at Arafat, with a company of other pilgrims, when an arm was projected into the

tent, and placed this dish before me, filled with sweetmeat. I sent out servants to see who had brought it to me, but no one was found."

A company of pilgrims arrived one year at Konieh on the return journey from Mekka, and after visiting all the famous men of the city they were conducted to Jelal's College. On seeing him seated there, they all exclaimed and fainted away. When they were recovered, Jelal began to offer excuses, saying to them, "I fear you have been deceived, either by an imposter, or by some person resembhng me in feature." The pilgrims, however, one and all objected. " Why talks he thus? " they said to one another. " Why strive to make us doubt our eyes? By the God of heaven and earth, he was with us in person, habited in the very dress he now wears, when we assumed the pilgrim garb at Mekka. He perfoimed with us all the ceremonies of the pilgrimage there, and at Arafat. He visited with us the tomb of the Prophet at Medina, though he never once ate or drank with us."

For further examples of the marvellous acts of Jelalu-'d-Din as recorded by Efiaki, I must refer the curious reader to the work itself.

Perhaps the most famous among the Saints of the Turkish Conquest was Hadji Bektash–" Bek-tash the Pilgrim "–before mentioned. He was a man of noble birth and great learning, his father having been the Seyyid Ibrahim Mokerrem of Khorassan. While yet a boy, he is said to have been distinguished for his devotion, never mixing with companions of his own age; and evinced in early youth an aversion to all worldly pursuits. His education was entrusted to the Sage, Lokman, one of the disciples of Achmet Youssouf, the Chief of the Sheikhs of Turkestan, and by him Hadji Bektash was " instructed in all the exoteric and esoteric sciences. Lokman bestowed on this favourite pupil the mantle of the Imam Jafer, which he had himself received from Achmet Youssouf. According to his biographers, Hadji Bektash declined all the dignities of ered him by his father, " who died a prince in Khorassan," and devoted himself to a life of seclusion. Forty years were passed by this saintly man in study, fasting, and prayer, until he at length arrived at such a degree of perfection that his soul during sleep, left his body and entered the World of Spirits, and he became filled with Mystic Science and Divine Knowledge." In obedience to the spiritually received command of Achmet Youssouf he went with Mohammed Bokhara and seven hundred Dervishes and other pious men and saints into Asia Minor in the train of the conquering Orchan.

It appears to be a point of honour with a Dervish to maintain that the Order of which he is a member is the most important of all the religious sects of Islam, and that its Founder is the greatest and holiest of all Pirs. The legends related of Hadji Bektash by his followers, however, go far to establish his supremacy over all rival Saints. Of these the following may serve as a specimen.

Hadji Bektash was one day sitting with some of his followers on a wall, when they saw a rival Dervish advancing towards them, mounted on a roaring lion, and holding in his hand as a whip, a writhing serpent with which he chastised his steed. The disciples, who had never before beheld such a sight, marvelled greatly; but their Sheikh calmly observed, My brethren, there is little merit in being able to ride upon a lion; I will show you a more wonderful thing. This wall on which we are sitting shall advance and bar the further progress of yon wild beast and his rider." The Dervishes immediately found that they were being carried forward by the wall towards the lion, whose rider was compelled to acknowledge the superior spiritual rank of Hadji Bekt h. Evliya Effendi relates in his Travels" that this wall, which was still in his day of large proportions, and even the identical spot on which the Saint was seated when he performed the miracle, was pointed out to him at Sari-beg in Asia Minor.

Michelet has remarked, with reference to the legends which have collected round the Saints of the Christian Calendar, that " the monks wrote them, but the people were their authors." And

" Les Moines les ecrivjrent, mais le peuple les faisait." La Sorciere, p. 15.

the same may be said of most of the extravagant stories related of Dervish Saints. In the following story, for instance, the Moslem Saint, Mohammed Bokhara, is made the hero of adventures evidently borrowed from a widespread Eastern folktale.

This Mohammed Bokhara, also called Sari Saltik and Kilgra Sultan, was one of the fighting saints of the Ottoman conquest, and a favourite disciple of Hadji Bektash. After the conquest of Broussa by Sultan Orchan (1326), the Master bestowed on his disciple the insignia of the Order–a wooden sword, a sheepskin mat, a banner, drum, and horn– and despatched him on a mission to the Unbelievers. The Saint and his seventy followers spread their sheepskins on the sea and sailed away, " with drums beating and banners flying, from Roumelia to the Crimea, from Muscovy to Poland." At Dantzic, Sari Saltik had an interview with Saint Nikola the Patriarch, whom he slew. Then, adopting his name and dress, he, as the Patriarch, travelled about Europe for some years, during which time he converted many thousands to the faith of Islam. The King of the Dobrudja, after listening to the preaching of the Saint, desired of him a miracle in confirmation of his mission. There happened to be then in the Dobrudja a terrible seven-headed Dragon, and the King's two daughters were doomed to be devoured by him. Sari Saltik agreed to slay the monster and deliver the princesses on condition that they became Moslems.

Accompanied by his seventy Dervishes, beating

THE ACTS OF THE ADEPTS 165 their drums and waving their banners, he proceeded to the column to which the doomed maidens were bound, drew his wooden sword, and waited. The Dragon soon appeared, and the Saint, addressing him with the passage from the Koran beginning " Greetings to Noah in Both Worlds," cut off three of his heads so that he fled away with the remaining four. The Dervish pursued him to his den, at the entrance to which he cut off the remaining heads, and then followed the monster into the cave, where a frightful struggle took place. The Dragon pressed the Saint so hard against the rock that the impression of his hands and feet remained visible. At last Sari Saltik slew the monster, and, with his bloody breast and bloody sword, he led the maidens back to their father, the king.

In the meantime, however, a " cursed (Christian) monk" who had shown Saltik the way to the column, had picked up the three tongues and the ears of the three heads first cut off and carried them to the king, boasting that he had killed the Dragon. The princesses bore out the testimony of the Saint; but the monk persisting in his statement. Sari Saltik proposed as a test that they should be both broiled together in a cauldron. The monk did not approve of this trial by ordeal; but, by command of the King, he was obuged to undergo it. Sari Saltik was tied up by his Dervishes, and the monk by his companions, and both were put into a large cauldron heated by an immense fire. It was at this hour that Hadji Bektash, who was then at 12–(2119)

Kir Shehir in Asia Minor, swept with a handkerchief a dripping rock, exclaiming, "My Saltik Mohammed is now in great distress, may Allah assist him! " Ever since that day, salt, instead of, as before, fresh water, has dripped from that rock, and from it the kind of salt called " Hadji Bektash " is produced. The cauldron being opened, Sari Saltik was found perspiring and ejaculating " O All Vivifying! (Yi Hayl) but of the monk nothing was left but blackened cinders and burnt bones. The King of the Dobrudja, moved by this miracle, instantly, together vith seven thousand of his subjects, embraced the faith of Islam. He also sent ambassadors to Sultan Orchan, who bestowed upon him the title of Kadi, a horse-tail standard, a banner, and the Moslem name of AU Mukhtar.

In the same year Sari Saltik made his will, wherein he commanded seven cofhns to be made, because seven Kings were to contend for his body after death. And so it fell out. After his corpse had been washed and laid in one of the coffins, seven kings demanded the privilege of burying it. A cofhn was given to all the seven, who were " the Kings of Muscovy, Poland, Bohemia, Sweden, Adrianople, Moldavia, and the Dobrudja." The last buried the coffin that fell to him in the Cave of the Dragon at Kilgra on the Black Sea, and built a Tekkeh close by, where the Saint's wooden sword, drum, and banner were treasured as rehcs.

1 One of the attributes of the Deity 2 Narrative of Travels.

THE ACTS OF THE ADEPTS 167

Of the many Dervish saints whose turbes or mausoleums are to be found in that picturesque old capital of the Ottoman Sultans, Broussa, one of the most famous was Shemsii-'d-Dm Mohammed Ben Ali, a Seyyid, or descendant of the Prophet, who also bore the honourable title of Emir Sultan, bestowed on him on account of his learning. When performing his pilgrimage to the holy cities, the Sherifs, his fellow descendants, refused him the portion to which he was entitled by his descent. The Saint accordingly decided to refer the matter to the decision of the Prophet himself, and, going to his tomb accompanied by the other Seyyids, they heard a voice from within cry " Health to thee, my son Mohammed Ben Ah! go to Riim with the lamp! " Upon hearing this, the Sherifs threw themselves at Shemsii-'d-Din's feet, and acknowledged their fault. He shortly afterwards set out for Anatolia, whereupon a lamp suspended from heaven became his guide on the way, and disappeared only when he entered the gates of Broussa. Emir Sultan accepted this as a sign that he was to take up his abode in this city, where he found awaiting him four hundred thousand disciples. For the inhabitants had seen the lamp hanging from heaven for three days, and knew by that wonder that they might expect the advent of a 1 Referred to on p. 33. gee note, p. 16.

3 This is evidently one of the characteristically Oriental exaggerations with which Evhya Effendi is frequently taxed by his translator.

Saint. Under his direction they all became Dervishes. Sultan Bayazid not only walked on foot by his stirrup, but gave him his daughter Nutiifer Hannm in marriage. When this Sultan had completed the building of the Oulou Jami, i qj- Great Mosque," he asked Emir Sultan if it were not a perfect mosque. " Yes, replied the Saint, " it is a very elegant mosque, but some cups of wine for the refreshment of the pious are wanting in the middle." The Sultan exclaimed with surprise, "How would it be possible to stain the house of Allah with the liquor forbidden by the law? " " Well," rephed the Saint, " thou hast built a mosque, Bayazid, and findest it strange to put z cup of wine therein; but thy body, which is a house of Allah more excellent than a talisman composed of the Divine Names, or the throne of Allah Himself–how is it that thou dost not fear to stain the purity of this godhke house with wine, day and night? " From that moment, adds the narrator, "Bayazid repented, and left off drinking wine."

Among the number of holy men who favoured Evliya Effendi with their friendship, was the Sheikh Abdi Dedeh, who built the Mevlevi Monastery at Kassim Pasha, on the outskirts of the capital.

1 Three Sultans took part in the building of this magnificent mosque, Murad I, Bayazid I, and Mohammed I. The interior is divided by pillars into twenty-five halls, each roofed with a separate dome. It is, however, not this " Great Mosque," but another that bears the name of " Bayazid Ilderim."

According to this author, Sheikh Abdi was "in mystic lore, a second Jelalij-'d-Din. He knew by their names all those who came to the convent, though he had never seen them before. When he sang, " he intoxicated all Dervishes." Evliya Effendi also narrates that, as Sultan Murad was on one occasion returning from Broussa to Constantinople by sea, he was in danger of being drowned near Cape Bozbournou, when he " saw at the ship's head the Sheikh, who calmed the waves."

Of the Saints canonized in our own days I may mention a Sheikh of Cavalla, whose gift of prophecy had enabled him to predict the day and hour of his departure from the world. This holy man caused his tomb to be prepared in the hall of the Tekkeh; and, though apparently in his usual health, he, on the eve of the appointed day, announced to his wife and his disciples that he must now take leave of them, as that day would be his last. These farewells taken, he calmly proceeded alone to the hall and lay down in the tomb that was to be his last resting-place. When, on the following morning, the disciples arrived at the Tekkeh, they found that their revered master had indeed, according to his prediction, breathed his last. The fame of his holy Hfe and the circumstances of his death soon became widely known in the neighbourhood; the devout watchers did not fail to see supernatural lights hovering over his grave; and before long miracles of heahng were reported to have been performed at the shrine of the Sheikh of Cavalla.

CHAPTER XI
WOMEN MYSTICS

Her Woman's sex dims not the Sun's effulgent ray; Though Mascuune the Moon, he lighteth not the day."

From the Arabic.

It is characteristic of the high estimation in which women have always been held by the Siifis that the place of honour among the early mystics is by them assigned to a woman. This distinguished person was

Rabia al Adawia, also called Umm al Khair (' The

Mother of Good,") a native of Bissora, who lived in the eighth century, and whose reputed grave on

Mount Tor, to the east of Jerusalem, became, like those of the generality of Moslem saints, a place of pilgrimage. The words and actions of this Queen of Mystics have been recorded by many Oriental writers, and contain a germ of Sufism, or kind of sentimental pantheism, which often found poetical or rhythmic expression. An eminent Siifi writer of the twelfth century, Ibn Khamis Al Juhani, relates in his works many anecdotes of Rabia's sanctity and piety, some of which are quoted by Ibn Khallikan in his Biographical Dictionary. The following verse is attributed to her:–

My heart I keep for Thy communion, Lord! And those who seek me but my body find. My guests may with my body converse hold, But my Belov'd alone holds converse with my heart.

1 In Arabic, as in German, the Moon is masculine and the Sun feminine.

2 M. Dozy, however, attaches no historical value to the legends concerning Rabia. Essai, etc., p. 318-19.

It is related that on one occasion the celebrated Moslem theologians, Hassan of Bassora and Shakik of Balk, came to visit this pious lady when she was ill. The former greeted her in mystic fashion with the following couplet:–

He in his faith cannot be all sincere.

Who mourns the chastening of his Master dear.

Shakik added, correcting his friend:–

He in his faith cannot be all sincere,

Who joys not, chastened by his Master dear.

Rabia's enthusiasm, however, went beyond that of her eminent and reverend guests, and she replied:–

He in his faith cannot be all sincere.

Who feels a smart when draws his Master near I

Another eminent contemporary theologian, Sofyan ath Thauri, exclaimed one day in her presence, "O what anguish is mine!" Rabia reproved him, saying, "Speak not a lie, but rather say, O how little anguish is mine! If thou wert really in affliction thou couldst not sigh." One of the Siifi brethren relates that in his prayers he was accustomed to invoke Rabia, who appeared to him in a vision, and said: Thy offerings were presented to us on trays of light, and covered with napkins of light." She often said, "If my good works appear to the world, I count them as nought," and one of her counsels was: " Hide thy good deeds as thou wouldst hide thy sins." One of her biographers gives a story as related by Abda, a handmaid of this pious lady: " Rabia used to pass the whole night in prayer, and at morning dawn she took a short sleep in her oratory till daylight; and I have heard her exclaim, springing from her couch as if in dread: 0 my soul! how long wilt thou sleep? When wilt thou awake? Soon thou shalt sleep to rise no more till the call shall summon thee on the Day of Resurrection! This was her constant custom till the day of her death. On its approach, she called me and said, O Abda! inform none of my death, and shroud me in this gown. This was a gown of hair-cloth which she wore when praying at the time when the eyes of others were closed in sleep. I shrouded her in that gown and in a woollen veil which she used to wear; and about a year afterwards I saw her in a dream, clothed in a gown and veil of green silk, the like of which for beauty I never beheld. And I said, O Rabia! what has become of the gown in which I shrouded thee, and of the woollen veil? To which she answered, By Allah! it was taken off me, and I received in exchange what thou seest on me; my shroud was folded up, a seal was put upon it, and it was taken up to the highest heaven, that by it my reward might be complete on the day of resurrection. It was for this, I observed, that thou didst work when in the world. ' And what is this, she rejoined, compared with what I have seen of Allah's bounty to his Saints? I asked her in what state was Obaida (a holy woman who had predeceased her), and she replied, It cannot be described. By Allah! She has surpassed us all, and reached the highest place in Paradise.

And how is that, said I, when all men considered thee far, far above her? ' Because, she rephed, when in the world she took no thought for the morrow, nor even for the coming night. ' In the Acts of the Adepts, and elsewhere, we also find records of many holy women, some of whom were honoured with the friendship of the poet-saint Jelalu-'d-Din; and not least eminent among them were his wife, Kira Khatun, and his daughter-in-law, Fatima. The latter had been taught to read and write by Jelal, who bestowed upon her the comphmentary title of his ' Right Eye "; her sister he called his " Left Eye "; and their mother, Latifa Khatiin, " the Personification of God's grace." "Fatima," says the story, "was a Saint, and continually worked miracles. She fasted by day, and watched by night, tasting food only once in three days. She was very charitable to the poor, the orphans, and the widows, distributing to them food and raiment."

Kira Khatun was also a most saintly woman. She was Jelalii-'d-Din's second wife, and survived him. When she, too, departed this hfe, and was about to be buried by the side of her husband, a strange incident occurred. As her corpse was being borne towards its last resting-place, the procession passed through one of the gates of the town (Konieh). Here the bearers found themselves arrested by some unseen power, so that they could not move hand or foot. This singular effect lasted for about half an hour. Her stepson, Sultan Veled, struck up a hymn and commenced a holy dance, after which the bearers recovered the use of their limbs and the interment was completed. That same night a holy man of the fraternity saw Kira Khatun in heaven by the side of her husband, and enquired of her the reason of the arrestation of the funeral. She informed him thus:–

" On the previous day a man and a woman had on that spot, been stoned to death for adultery. I took compassion on them, interceded for their forgiveness, and obtained for them admission to Paradise. My preoccupation on their behalf was the reason of the delay met with by the funeral procession."

According to Eflski, there hved at Konieh in the days of Jelslii-'d-Din, a saintly lady named Fakhrii-n-Nisa (" The Glory of Women "), who enjoyed the acquaintance of the holy men of the time,

" The Mesnevi, p. 119. This curious legend appears to illustrate the Moslem notion that the soul remains with the body until after burial, and that it is only then–except, perhaps, in the case of such saintly persons as Kira Khatun–that its ultimate destiny is decided. After the last rites have been performed by the relatives, the Imam is left alone by the grave in order, it is said, to prompt the deceased in his replies to the Questioners." These are the two Angels, Mounkir and Nekir, who, according to Moslem belief, enter the grave with the dead in order to interrogate them concerning their faith. If the dead has been a devout Moslem, his reply will be " My God is Allah; my Prophet, Mohammed; my religion, Islam; and my Kibla, the Kaaba." If, however, he has been but an indifferent follower of the Prophet, he will not be able to remember this formula.

all of whom were aware of her sanctity. Miracles were wrought by her in countless numbers. She constantly attended the meetings at Jelal's house and received occasionally visits from him. Her friends suggested that she ought to go and perform the pilgrimage to Mekka; but she wordd not decide upon so serious an undertaking without first consulting Jelal. Accordingly, she went to see him. As she entered his presence, before she spoke, he called out to her: " Oh most happy idea! May thy journey be prosperous! God willing, we shall be together." She bowed, but said nothing. The disciples present were puzzled. "That night she remained a guest at Jelal's house, conversing with him till past midnight, when, according to his custom, he went to perform his devotions on the housetop. Presently he called to her to come up also, and when she did so, she saw the holy Kaaba of Mekka revolving in the air above the head of Jelal. So overcome was Fakhrii-n-Nisa by this wondrous sight, that she sank down in a swoon. On recovering she came to the conclusion that it was not necessary for her to undertake the difficult and dangerous journey to the Holy City, as its chief attraction had been thus marvellously revealed to her."

In later centuries also it would appear that Societies of pious women have been from time to time afhhated with the Dervish Orders. These holy women are frequently mentioned in the biographies of Dervish Saints, either individually, or collectively by some such name as " The Sisters of Riim," alluded to in the writings of Hadji Bektash. Nor is such mystical devotion entirely unknown among Osmanh women at the present day. The widow of the Cavalla Sheikh above referred to, a woman of great intelhgence, presided, after her husband's death, over a society of female devotees who held their meetings at her residence. A British subject who had had business relations with the Sheikh in connection with the tobacco-growing industry of Cavalla and the neighbourhood, from which the revenues of the Tekkeh were derived, obtained from this lady many curious details concerning her Sisterhood, and was even allowed by her to be a hidden spectator of their devotions. During the first years of my residence at Salonica I chanced to come into contact with a Turkish lady who was always referred to as " the Dervish Hanum, and enjoyed the reputation of being no mean poetess. Though sufficiently liberal minded to admit European ladies to her acquaintance and visit them in their own houses, she, however, always skilfully parried any attempt to ehcit information with respect to the Sisterhood of Mystics of which report proclaimed her to be a distinguished member.

In the earher times of Islam much greater freedom of manners appears to have existed than has been the case in later centuries. Indeed the records of the Prophet's commands on the subject of the seclusion of women, and the glimpses we have in the Koran and in the writings of the Commentators DERVISH WITH LEANING CRUTCH of the social life of his time, do not point to any greater " subjection of women " than that enjoined by the Apostle Paul; and the women of the Prophet's household evidently held a much higher position, and were treated with far more respect than are the women of a provincial Armenian family at the present day. The Turkish harem system, though less rigid than is generally believed in Europe, naturally offers great obstacles to the formation of sisterhoods. And the natural result of denying to women any social intercourse with the other sex has been to stifle any desire for even that moderate amount of education necessary to enable them to read and appreciate the spiritual writings by which their husbands and brothers are influenced. For though it is naturally the more ignorant among Moslem women who believe most implicitly in the wonderworking powers of Dervish Sheikhs, it is on the other hand only women who have received a good Turkish education who " enter on the Mystic Path, and are distinguished by the title of Sufi Hanuni,

CHAPTER XII
STATUS AND INFLUENCE OF THE ORDERS

"Not at Strife's door sits he; when thwarted neer Starts up to contest; all unmoved his soul, He is no Saint who from the Path would stir Though a huge rock should from a mountain roll."

After the establishment of the twelve original Orders, the numbers of the Dervishes greatly increased in all the Asiatic countries which had come under the influence of Islam. In the train of Ala-'d-Din, Sultan of Iconium, and his successor Orchan, they spread themselves over Asia Minor; and, after the conquest of Broussa by the latter prince, the munificence of the victors, who attributed the success of their armies to the presence of these holy men, enabled the Dervish Sheikhs to found monasteries and colleges in all parts of the Empire. For the Founders, at least, of these early Orders were, as has been seen, men of great learning and wide culture, as well as of saintly life.

The slopes of the Bithynian Olympus rising steeply behind the ancient Ottoman capital of Broussa, which had for centuries previously been the resort of Christian hermits and cenobites, were now taken possession of by Moslem recluses who here established themselves among the flocks of the Turcoman nomads; and the coolness and quiet of the retreats which had favoured the holy idleness of

Christian monks, now charmed the reveries of Dervish poets and the meditations of Siifi philosophers. Their honoured tombs may still be seen at the foot of the mountain where they passed their lives, or in the vicinity of the Schools of Philosophy in which they taught. Amid these beautiful and romantic surroundings, after having themselves drunk deeply of the wells of science, they spread their sentiments, their ideas, and their knowledge in works which will live as long as the Ottoman language and nation endure. Sultan Orchan, who acknowledged that he had conquered Broussa by their spiritual aid, placed the most distinguished among the Sheikhs at the head of the Schools he founded, endowed them with liberal salaries, and honoured them with complimentary titles.

The influence exercised by the Dervishes over the minds of the people generally, though often, as we have seen, made use of by the Sultans and their Ministers for State purposes, has occasionally caused alarm, and the Orders have in consequence not only been at such times regarded with suspicion, but subjected to active persecution. The earliest, and in fact, the general, accusation brought against these mystics was that their practices were contrary to the spirit of Islam and the express commands of the Prophet; and from the time of their first formation, under the Khalifs, attempts were made to stop the progress of this enthusiasm for a monastic life. In these attempts the civil power had the entire concurrence of the Ulema or Legists who, as students and expounders of the Koranic Law, found their own spiritual supremacy menaced, and were naturally jealous of the growing influence and importance of this rival sect. Under the pretence of defending Moslem orthodoxy, but in reahty to maintain their own power and prestige, they became the formidable auxiharies of the government in a struggle which menaced at one time the throne itself. But the active opposition to the Dervishes appears always to have been rather spasmodic and intermittent than regular and systematic; and what ground they lost at one period and under one sovereign they often more than regained under his successor. In the nineteenth century, as in the days of Orchan, their influence has been made use of by Sultans and Generals to excite the zeal and courage of their troops in battle. Whenever a mihtary campaign had been organised, a number of Dervishes from nearly all the Orders hasten to join the army. Commanding officers gladly engage their services and treat them with every respect and consideration, as their presence in the camp, where they spend whole days and nights fasting in their tents, while offering supphcations and making vows for the success of the arms of the True Believers, maintains a most desirable religious enthusiasm among the troops. On the eve of an action the Dervishes roam excitedly through the camp, rehearsing the benefits promised by the Prophet to all who fight for the Faith of Islam, or who die in

Ubicini, Lettres sur la Turqiiie, Vol, I, p. 166, arms, and seek to rouse the zeal and animate the courage of the soldiers by every means in their power. During a battle their excitement increases, and their voices may be heard above the din of war, shouting, 'O Victors!" (Yd Ghazi) "O Martyrs!" Yd Shahid) 'Yd Allah ' or Yd Hoo! " (0 Him). If they fancy the Holy Standard, the mantle of the Prophet, to be in danger, they crowd round the sacred reuc to strengthen the hues of the officers stationed as its guard, and not only sustain their efforts, but themselves perform prodigies of valour. A Dervish of high renown in his day, Ak Shemsu-'ddin by name, is said to have foretold to Mohammed "the Conqueror" the day and hour of the fall of Constantinople. Together with seventy-seven other " distinguished and holy men beloved of Allah," he accompanied the Sultan to that memorable siege; and the Sultan made a covenant with them that one half of the city should belong to them and the other half to the Moslem conquerors. " And I wiu," said he, " build for each of you a monastery, an almshouse, a college, and a School of Sacred Traditions Dar-1-Hadis)" The deeds of valour achieved by these enthusiasts at the taking of Constantinople, and the miracles performed in answer to their prayers are recorded–and, it need hardly be said, exaggerated–by Moslem historians; and the tombs of many are to this day places of pilgrimage for the Faithful.

Nor were the Dervishes held in less honour by succeeding Sultans. After the capture of the 13–(aiig)

Byzantine capital and the consolidation of the Empire, their poets and writers remained in high favour at Court, and there were few Padishahs who were not enrolled as members of one or more of the Orders. The long reign of Bayazid II (1481-1521) also bears traces of the influence of Mystic philosophy on the Court. The most renowned Dervish of that time, the Sheikh Jasi, had, when about to start on a pilgrimage to Mekka, foretold to Bayazid, then governor of Amasia, that on his return from the Holy City he would find the Prince on the throne, and it fell out as he had predicted. This eminent man received the titles of " Sheikh of Sultans," and " Sultan of Sheikhs," and his cell was the meeting-place of all the dignitaries of the Empire. The Turkish writers Seadeddin and Ali narrate the biographies of thirty eminent Dervishes who flourished in the reign of this Sultan, called by many Ottoman historians " Bajazid the Siifi." The influence of the Dervish society by which this Sultan surrounded himself may also be seen in his poetry, which breathes a spirit of mysticism and philosophy markedly absent from the writings of his talented but unhappy brother, Prince Djem, and his son, Selim I.

Notwithstanding the secular hostility of the Ulema, it does not appear that, previous to the 16th century, the Dervish Orders were interfered with by the Government. For so long as the substance of the doctrines held by the higher grades of these mystics was kept secret, the denunciations by the Legists of their ascetic practices, their vows, the dancing and other peculiar exercises performed in their Tekkehs, their pretensions to miraculous gifts, and claims to direct communion with the Deity, had but httle effect. But as the influence and prestige of the Dervishes increased, many of the Orders relaxed by degrees the prudence and severity of their original rules, and allowed much of their doctrine to become pubhcly known. Their enemies were now enabled to make definite and serious charges against them. They were accused of attempting to make innovations on the dogmas of Islam; of following practices forbidden by the Koran; of denying the very existence of a personal Allah; of teaching disrespect for all estabhshed institutions; and of setting at nought all law, both human and divine. Their religious exercises were denounced as profane acts; and it was asserted that all kinds of abominable practices were indulged in by them in the seclusion of their monasteries. The general tendency of the Dervish institutions appeared to the Ulema to threaten also the introduction into Islam of something analogous to the " Holy Priesthood " and " Apostolic Succession " of the Romish Church–ideas utterly at variance with the spirit of the Koran. An alleged discovery that gave a still greater shock to the orthodox mind was that the Dervishes concluded some of their prayers by anathematising the Ommiade Khahfs and glorifying the Khahf Ali; and, consequently, that, though nominally Silnnis, they virtually belonged to the heterodox sect of the Skids.

There seems, however, Uttle reason to doubt that whenever overt hostihty has been manifested against the Dervish Orders by a Sultan and his Ministers it has invariably been prompted by pohtical, rather than religious motives. For notwithstanding the odium cast upon these Mystics by the Legists, no active measures, as above remarked, appear to have been taken against them by the Government until the beginning of the sixteenth century, when political events caused them to be looked upon as a possible source of danger to the State.

A new dynasty had been founded in Persia at this period on the basis of rehgion. The Sufi Philosophy had always been popular in that country; and Persia was at the same time the stronghold of the Shia heresy and of the Dervish Fraternities. A Dervish Sheikh, named Eidar, who traced his descent from the Khahf Ah, having gained a great reputation for sanctity and a numerous following of disciples and adherents, assumed the title of " Sufi" par excellence, and declared himself to have been commissioned by Allah to work a religious reformation. Sheikh Eidar perished in the attempt; but his young son, Ismail, was protected by his faithful disciples, who took refuge with him in Ghilsn, and carefully trained him in his father's principles. In 1501, at the head of a numerous body of partisans, Ismail revived the claims of Sheikh Eidar; and, gradually overcoming all opposition, he at length became the founder of the Sufi Dynasty, and the ruler of an extensive Empire.

His doctrines gained also many adherents in the Asiatic provinces of the Ottoman Empire, where Sehm I took early and vigorous measures to suppress this new heretical sect. For, as Church and State are, in Islam, identical, a blow aimed at the one menaces equally the other; and the great schism of the Sunnis and Shids is not a mere diversity of opinion purely religious and theoretic, but also a practical political dispute concerning the succession to the Khalifate, the headship of the Moslem Faith. Sultan Selim, whose inquisitorial talents are celebrated by Ottoman historians, organised a system of secret police by means of which he caused to be made out a list of all his subjects belonging to the Sufi sect. Their number amounted to seventy thousand, forty thousand of whom were massacred, the rest being imprisoned for life. In Damascus a few hours sufficed for the extermination of the whole community of schismatic Mahommedans. The Persian monarch shortly afterwards declared war against the destroyer of his co-religionists, and a sanguinary campaign ensued. The Ottoman Dervishes in European Turkey, whose Shid tendencies were more than suspected, were, very naturally, looked upon with disfavour during the course of these events, the Ulema making the most of this favourable opportunity by exciting the minds of the populace as well as of the authorities against their rivals.

A new sect, created about the beginning of the sixteenth century by Sheikh Hamza and called after him the Hamzavis, appears to have been, from its very foundation, in bad repute with the orthodox; and Sheikh Hamza was arrested and subsequently executed by order of the Sheikh-ul-Islam, the ostensible charge against him being that he omitted to repeat at his devotions the obhgatory number of the Isma i Sherif, or " Praises of the Prophet." By the rest of the Dervishes he was naturally regarded as a martyr, and his reputation for piety and extraordinary powers still survives in the capital. Another Sheikh of the same Order was also put to death shortly afterwards on an accusation of heterodoxy, together with forty of his disciples, who appear to have voluntarily given themselves up to the authorities. And so great was the effervescence of the orthodox under several succeeding reigns, and particularly in that of Mohammed IV, that the Ulema and other rigid Mohammedans even ventured to propose the extermination of all the Orders, the confiscation of their revenues, and the destruction of their monasteries. An attempt was, indeed, made by the Grand Vizier of that Sultan, Achmet Kiupruh, to suppress the Bektashi, Khalvetti, Djelvetti, and Shemshi Orders. Like all former and subsequent attempts, however, it succeeded but partially, as the Government was overawed by the Janisseries, whose intimate connection with the Bektashi Order made them the auies of the Dervishes generally, and the Porte feared to do anything that might arouse the resentment of this formidable force.

The action of the Sultans, too, seems to have been but half-hearted; for it is recorded that even Sehm I,– whom Mouradja DOhsson describes as " poet, parricide and fratricide, mystic, tyrant, and conqueror,"–made pilgrimages to the tombs of deceased, and to the cells of living Sheikhs of repute; and that he raised at Damascus a mosque over the grave of the eminent saint, Muhajjin el Arabi. Suleyman I also built at Konieh, in honour of Jelalii-'d-Din, a mosque, a Tekkeh, and public alms-kitchen. At Sidi Ghazi he erected a great estabushment with a Tekkeh and college for the Bektashis, and he also repaired the Tekkeh covering the tomb of Abdul Kadr Ghilani, the sainted founder of the Kadiri Order, thus drawing upon himself the benedictions of three influential Orders.

After this stormy period the Orders appear to have enjoyed a long interval of free-dom from persecution. For Evliya Effendi, writing towards the end of the seventeenth century, makes no mention of the existence of any popular ill-feeling towards the Dervishes with whom he was closely connected during the whole of his long and adventurous life. The massacre of the Janisseries by Mahmoud II, the " Reformer," in the beginning of last century, was, however, followed by persecution of the Bektashi Order, who were suspected of having been concerned in the revolts that ensued. Its members were accused of treason against the State, and the chief Legists agreed with the Sultan that a severe

Histoire de VEmpire Ottomane, Part I, p. 377.

sentence should be passed upon the Brotherhood. Its three principal Sheikhs were consequently publicly executed; the Order was declared abohshed, many of its Tekkehs were destroyed, and its members generally were banished from the capital, those who remained being compelled to abandon their distinctive dress.

This determined action on the part of the Government spread consternation through-out the Dervish Orders in the Empire, whose members feared for the moment that they, Hke the Bektashis, were all doomed to destruction or dispersion; and, to use the expressive Oriental phrase, "They remained motionless, expecting their last day, devoured by anguish, and with their backs resting against the wall of stupefaction." But here Sultan Mahmoud paused in his work of destruction. " Though "–to use the metaphors of the historian of the massacre of the Janisseries–" he had not feared to open with the sword a road for pubhc happiness by cutting down the thorny bushes that obstructed his progress and tore his imperial mantle," he hesitated to decree the entire destruction of institutions which had enjoyed the respect and devotion of his predecessors and of Moslems generally for upwards of a thousand years. This " hesitation," is, however, not so surprising when we learn the 1 Ubicini, Leitres sur la Turquie, Vol. I, p. 107.

2 Ubicini, who stigmatises the doctrines of the Sufis as "abominable," appears to regret that the Dervishes were not then destroyed root and branch. See his Lettres, etc. Vol. I, pp. 101 and 114-115.

fact, of which Ubicini appears to have been ignorant, that Sultan Mahmoud was an affiuated member of the Mevlevi Tekkeh at Pera, and frequently visited it; and that he also honourcd with his presence the meetings of a Nakshibendi fraternity estabhshed in the suburb of Foundouldi.

The Dervishes, however, on finding that the blow dealt at the Bektsshis was not followed by the suppression or even persecution of the other Orders, soon recovered from their consternation; and the more fanatical among them set on foot a secret agitation with the object of inciting the populace against a Sultan who had dared to raise his hand against the chosen of Allah." In 1837 Mahmoud narrowly escaped falhng a victim to the frenzied zeal of one of these ascetics. As he was crossing the Bridge of Galata, surrounded by his escort, a long-haired cenobite, commonly known in the capital as " The Hairy Sheikh," darted from among the bystanders, and, seizing the bridle of the Sultan's horse, exclaimed, "Giaour Padishah! (Infidel Sultan!) Art thou not yet satiated with abominations? Thou Shalt answer to Allah for thy impieties. Thou destroyest the institutions of thy Brethren; thou ruinest Islam, and drawest down the wrath of Allah on thyself and on the nation! " The Sultan, fearing that popular feehng might be roused against himself by the ascetic's denunciations, commanded his guards to remove the madman from his path. " Madman! " echoed the infuriated Dervish.

John Brown, The Dervishes, p. 346-347 n.

"Sayest thou that I am mad? The spirit of Allah, which inspires me, and which I must obey, has commanded me to declare His truth, and promised me the reward of the Faithful! " The fanatic was, however, seized and put to death without delay. His body was given up to his brethren, who buried it with the honours due to a martyr; and on the following day a report was circulated that the watchers had seen a Nur, or supernatural hght, hovering over the grave of the Sheikh–a convincing proof of the favour with which Allah had regarded his action.

It needed, however, a bold reformer to put a noisy fanatic to death, and the majority of Sultans and statesmen have contented themselves with exihng to some remote part of the Empire a Dervish whose influence on the populace they had cause to fear.

Generally speaking, whenever public hostihty has been excited against the Dervish Orders it has had its foundation in the horror with which the orthodox Sunni Mohammedans regard the Shid heresy, and this hostility seems never to have been very general or of long continuance. For those whose religious principles and devotion to the purity of the creed of Islam incited them to combat the growing power of the Dervishes, have invariably been, in their turn, combated by other principles drawn from the same source; the majority of the Turkish nation having always regarded the Dervishes, their Sheikhs, and, above all, the Founders of the Orders, as the beloved Sons of Heaven, and in intimate relations with spiritual powers. These opinions have for basis the tradition that the different Orders originated, as above mentioned, in the two congregations of Abu Bekr and AH, and that the grace bestowed upon them by the Prophet, both as his relations and Vicars, had been miraculously transmitted through the series of Sheikhs who, from age to age, have governed the monastic societies. It is also popularly beheved that the legion of Saints, constituting the Mohammedan spiritual hierarchy alluded to in a previous chapter as perpetually existing among mankind, are to be found among the members of the Dervish fraternities. Consequently, to condemn, persecute, and destroy them, as was the unanimous cry of the Legists, would have been to draw upon the whole nation the wrath of all the holy Saints. Even the less enthusiastic did not dare openly to declare themselves hostile to the Dervishes.

Moslems generally respect what is beyond their comprehension, and hold this mixture of rehgious practices and profane exercises to be a mystery which the True Behever should treat with silent and unquestioning reverence. And the superstitious ideas which these ascetics have the talent to perpetuate in their nation have always served as their shield. So persistent, too, is the influence of, and veneration for, the spiritual character of the more eminent among the Sheikhs, that even those Ottomans whose education and intercourse with Europeans might be supposed to have freed them

from national superstition, are often found to be still under the influence of the ideas inculcated in youth. This is forcibly illustrated by an incident which was related to me during my sojourn at Salonica.

A Pasha, who had represented his Government at Paris, and whose sprightly wit, liberal ideas, and pleasant manners had, in his younger days, rendered him a great favourite in European circles, was appointed in after years to the governorship of the Vilayet of Broussa. During his residence in Europe he had collected a fine library, which he rightly considered the greatest ornament of his konak. But these reputed " infidel " writings gave umbrage to a fanatical old Dervish Sheikh of that city, who had great influence with the Pasha, and he resolved upon their destruction. With persuasive eloquence and prophetic promises, he so worked upon the mind of the Governor-General, that this dignitary was finally prevailed upon to consent to the destruction of his hterary treasures, and, hke those of Don Quixote, they were committed to the flames. The promised reward of this sacrifice was the much-desired and long-coveted post of Grand Vizier. Strange to say, the Pasha was actually called upon to occupy that high ofiice, though he retained it only for the brief period of three days.

From the earliest times to the present, the most general, though at the same time the most harmless, weapon used against the Dervishes has been that of ridicule. Turkish and Persian literature teems with satires, in proverb and story, on their peculiarities of dress and practice. Even the mystic Sadi does not spare them in his epigrams, though his satire is chiefly directed against those who are Dervishes in outward appearance only, as for instance:–

Of what avail is frock or rosary, Or clouted garment? Keep thyself but free From evil deeds, it will not need for thee To wear the " Crown " of felt, a Dervish be In heart, and wear the cap of Tartary.

A humorous story is current in the capital of a Dervish whose ass, a present from his Sheikh, died soon after he had set out on his pilgrimage. He buried the animal by the roadside, and giving out that a deceased companion was the occupant of the newly-made grave, soon obtained from the charitable passers-by sufficient funds to erect a turbeh over it, of which he constituted himself the guardian. Years passed. The turbeh became a great place of pilgrimage; miracles were performed at it, and the fame of the rival shrine reached the ears of the old Sheikh, who had heard no news of his pupil since his departure, and lamented him as dead. One day, accordingly, he locked up his turbeh in order to pay a visit to his brother Sheikh. He was hospitably received, and recognised the rival turbedji as his former disciple. When evening came, and the last of the pilgrims visiting the shrine had departed, the old Sheikh asked, with much curiosity,, who was the saint buried below, as he knew of none formerly residing in that part of the country. After some hesitation. Sheikh Ali confessed that his dead ass was the only occupant of the tomb. x s his superior did not seem much disturbed by the announcement, the younger Dervish ventured to enquire who was the Saint buried under his master's turbeh, and learnt at length that it was no other than the parent of his own sainted donkey 1 The most wildly fanatical are found among the wandering Dervishes, who, by their prophecies and adjurations, often excite the Moslem population against their Christian neighbours. Shortly before the outbreak of the troubles in Bulgaria in 1876, one of these zealots completely terrorised the Christian inhabitants of Adrianople. He knocked at one door after another in the Christian quarter, forced his way in when they were opened, and declared to the startled inmates that Allah had revealed to Him his desire that the infidels of the town should be destroyed within three days after Easter. He finally reached the house of the Bishop, to whom he repeated his menacing prophecy. The reverend gentleman, apprehensive of the possible consequences to his flock of these " revelations, went at once to inform the Governor-General of the incident. The Dervish was sent for, asked if he had said what was reported of him, and what he meant by it. The wily ascetic, however, merely shrugged his shoulders and replied carelessly that, as he was in his Hal when he made the alleged declaration, he was not responsible for anything he might have said. The Governor-General deemed it prudent to send him out of the city under escort with orders for his conveyance to Broussa; but the Dervish managed to elude the vigilance of his guards–possibly with their connivance–and continued his fanatical mission in other parts of the province.

WORKS REFERRED TO IN THE FOREGOING PAGES

Ali Aziz Effendi, of Crete. The Story of Jewad, translated by
E. J. W. GibB. 16 Brown, J. B. The Dervishes. 18, 37, 149, 187 Browne, E. G. A Year Among the Persians, 57-59 Clermokt-Ganneau. Revu6 Archeologique, 22n, Creasy, Sir E. S. History of the Ottoman Turks. 19 Cunningham-Graham, Mrs. Life of St. Theresa, 69n. DOhsson. Tableau GSnsrale de la Turquie, 2n., 187 Dozy. Essai sur IIslamisme, 5n., 14 Evliya Effendi, Narrative of Travels (Oriental Translation Fund), 28, 33, 39, 40, 72, 166, 187 Falconer, Prof. The Mesnevi, translation of, 55 Garcin de Tassy. M antic Uttair, translation of the, 5n., 49 Gaston Paris. Acad, des Inscriptions. 22n GibB, E. J. W. Ottoman Poems. 61-3, 119n. Griffith. Translation of Jami's Yusuf and Zulaihha, 56n., 59, 60 GuyARD. Revus de VHistoire des Religions, 22n. J AMI. Yusuf and Zulaikha: Salaman and Absal. 1, 56-60 jeLALtj-D-Din. The Mesnevi or Masnavi, 50-55; 110 Jones, Sir Wm. The Works, vol. i, p. 52 Lane. The Modern Egyptians. 35 Malcolm. History of Persia, 15, 153-4 MichELET. La Sorcidre, 163 Redhouse, Sir J. The Mesnevi; The Acts of the Adepts, translations of, 31n., 51n., 69, 91, 156, 158, 161, 174 Riley, Athelstan. Mount Athos. lln. Rozenzweig. Yusuf und Zulaikha, 56n. Sadi. The Gulistan, 35n. Sale. Al Koran, 72, 136 8, 143, 158 Silvestre de Sacy. Journal des Savants. 2n. Sprenger. Journal of the Asiatic Society, 5n. Ubicini. Lettres sur la Turquie, 46, 180, 188 Vaughan. Hours with the Mystics, 5n.
14–(3II9)
Aashik Pasha, mystical poetry of, 60

40 Ya Hoo

Lightning Source UK Ltd.
Milton Keynes UK
UKOW02f1725020615

252771UK00001B/127/P